A ROMP THROUGH THE BIBLE

Copyright 1987 by William R. Phillippe

Printed in the United States of America

10 9 8 7 6 5 4 3 2

Library of Congress Cataloging-in-Publication Data

Phillippe, William R., 1930-
    A romp through the Bible.

    1. Bible--Criticism, interpretation, etc. I. Title.
BS511.2.P52 1987   220.6   87-11618

ISBN 0-940473-01-1 hardbound
ISBN 0-940473-02-X paperback

A ROMP
THROUGH
THE BIBLE

William R. Phillippe

Wᵐ CAXTON LTD   917 FOSTER STREET   EVANSTON, IL 60201

A congregation has always been very important to me as a place where I have been nurtured, sheltered, and inspired. I wish to express special appreciation to the people of:

Bower Hill Community Church, Pittsburgh, PA;

Grosse Pointe Memorial Church, Grosse Pointe, MI;

Central Presbyterian Church, Summit, NJ; and

First Presbyterian Church, Lake Forest, IL

who have patiently listened, helpfully questioned, and gently taught me as we shared a ministry. I also want especially to thank:

Catherine, who has watched so many drafts go by;

Ann Hardy, whose keen interest in this book most directly led to its publication;

Dorothy Anderson for her careful correction of the manuscript; and

Ridgely W. Davis and Leonard Bennett for their design suggestions.

Table of Contents

Preface

This book is the result of many years of sharing with laypersons my love of the Bible. Like most people, I learned Bible stories at home and in the church; but I never caught sight of the whole thing. No one ever put together for me the amazing kaleidoscope of prophets, historians, storytellers, and visionaries who tell of their own encounters with life and God in the Bible.

I was fortunate in having a seminary professor who was at ease with the Old Testament and who taught me the pleasures of seeing these books through the eyes of those who wrote them. Far too often, even clergy look at the vital, humorous, emotion-packed writings of the Bible through the eyes of pale and juiceless theologians who lived insulated lives and viewed the world quite myopically. Such scholars sometimes seem afraid to enjoy either their own lives or the lives of the great saints and heroes of the Church.

The question, then, is whether WE can become free enough to read and enjoy the Bible. Can we see see it like Alice experienced her Wonderland in *Through the Looking Glass*. Alice was able to go through the mirror and walk around talking, joking, and living with the characters of another world. That is what I suggest we do together. So come with me on this journey through the printed pages, past the cold words, and into the amazing land of the Bible. Come face-to-face with men and women who felt the very touch of God in the midst of their lives and who were simple and honest enough to claim it with integrity. It just may make you aware that the same has happened in your own life.

In the past, the Church has had a great deal to say in formal ways about how we should approach the study of the Bible. In 1643 the "Westminster Divines" put it in this language:

> Although the light of nature, and the works of creation and providence, do so far manifest the goodness, wisdom, and power of God, as to leave men inexcusable; yet are they not sufficient to give that knowledge of God, and of his will, which is necessary unto salvation; therefore, it pleased the Lord, at sundry times, and in

diverse manners, to reveal himself, and to declare that his will unto his church; and afterwards for the better preserving and propagating against the corruption of the flesh, and the malice of Satan and of the world, to commit the same wholly unto writing; which maketh the Holy Scripture to be most necessary; those former ways of God's revealing his will unto his people being now ceased.[1]

For centuries this stilted language guided members of the Church in their study of the Bible, and, quite frankly, it seems to have prevented many from feeling its vitality.

In 1967 the United Presbyterian Church in the U.S.A. adopted a new confession using more intelligible language and expressing a more realistic view:

The Scriptures, given under the guidance of the Holy Spirit, are nevertheless the words of men, conditioned by the language, thought forms, and literary fashions of the places and times at which they were written. They reflect views of life, history, and the cosmos which were then current. The church, therefore, has an obligation to approach the Scriptures with literary and historical understanding. As God has spoken his word in diverse cultural situations, the Church is confident that he will continue to speak through the Scriptures in a changing world and in every form of human culture.[2]

In *A Declaration of Faith,* the Presbyterian Church U.S. stated:

Led by the Spirit of God, the People of Israel and of the early church preserved and handed on the story of what God has said and done in their midst and how they had responded to him. These traditions were often shaped and reshaped by the uses to which the community put

[1] The Westminster Confession of Faith, Chapter I, 1.

[2] The Confession of 1967, I, C, 2.

them. They were cherished, written down, and collected
as the holy literature of the people of God. [3]

This progressive understanding within the formal sanctions of
the Church has helped many of us boldly and publicly to declare our
love of the Bible. With my integrity intact, I now can say openly
that I take the Bible seriously but not literally. Further, I can
raise the question of the "negative space" in the Bible; that is,
what does the Bible NOT say? What perceptions are NOT recorded
from that long period of time?

On a shelf before me in my study is the work of historians
Will and Ariel Durant. In eleven volumes of 8,947 large pages they
have attempted to capture the history of the human race from its
misty beginnings to the death of Napoleon in 1821. Leafing through
my Bible, I am startled to realize that it contains over 2,000 years
of history in one relatively slim volume. Someone once calculated
that all the recorded words of Jesus could be read in less than an
hour, yet he taught for three years.

If, then, we realize that the Bible covers a period of about two
thousand years--that is, from Abraham and Sarah to the writings of
the early Church--and then relate that to world history, it's like
trying to tell the history of humankind from Julius Caesar to Nikita
Khruschev. Think of the variety there is within THAT story. Well,
the variety is just as great in our sacred history, but we have very
few words to work with. Again, ask what was not recorded? What
words, thoughts, dreams, and desires were left out?

Yet, it is an amazing collection of the full range of human
emotion: of birth and death; of murder, rape, war, and jealousies; of
visions and hymns of hope; of ventures of faith. As we will see
even in this very concentrated telling of our holy story we get a
fairly complete picture of the actors on that stage of history. In
the Old Testament particularly there are sections where the air
brush has not been applied to remove the warts and blemishes of
these searching humans in action and at rest. It is the story of
women and men discovering the nature of God.

On sheets of papyri the ancient Hebrew scribes captured the
lore of their people. These rolls of papyrus, known as biblia or
little books, comprise one of the most eloquent and comprehensive

---

[3] A Declaration of Faith, Chapter VI, 3.

accounts of an ancient people. For many of us it is the story of our mothers and fathers in the faith.

These literary artists were not just historians, editors and biographers, but impressive storytellers as well. With simple, vigorous, and concrete words they told a powerful story and described magnificent feats of leadership. Sometimes they soared with a poetic genius as they dealt with universal themes and touched the root of all humankind. At other times they lapse into a boring recital of ritual laws and genealogical tables.

But overall the Bible comes through as a record with considerable integrity, biased at many points, but with a bias that can be grasped and understood. We must constantly see it as something from the past, reflecting the past, conditioned by the thought forms of people quite different from us.

But, finally, it is not enough just to study the findings of scholars and archaeologists. It takes creative imagination to read and understand the lives, thoughts, and teachings of those ancient people. But it is worth the effort.

On various occasions I have gone into art museums to stand in awe before some of the great paintings of the world. Even if I had seen reproductions and read commentaries on them, I felt I could not say that I knew a picture until I had stood in the gallery and seen it for myself. But, I have discovered that even when I stood before them, the whole of those canvases was not revealed to me. If I go back to the gallery again and again, I come to know the painting better. As I stand before it and continue to study it, I learn something about the artist and the experiences out of which the painting grew. Only as I learn something of the circumstances surrounding its execution and the significance of the composition and other elements do I truly begin to see and understand the picture.

The point is obvious. People need to read the Bible for themselves. A reputable translation by good scholars in modern language is necessary. I use *The Jerusalem Bible* for the Old Testament and the *New English Bible* for the New Testament. Do not just read this book or some other book about the Bible. It is necessary to read the book itself.

> Within this awful volume lies
> The mystery of mysteries;
> Happiest they of human race

To whom their God has given grace
To read, to fear, to hope, to pray,
To lift the latch, to force the way;
But better had they ne'er been born,
That read to doubt, or read to scorn. [4]

William R. Phillippe
Lake Forest, IL 1987

---

[4] Sir Walter Scott, "The Monastery."

Introduction

First and foremost, this is a ROMP through the Bible. A romp is defined as "a fast but enforced pace," and another definition of romp is "to play boisterously." You will find that my intention is not only to move you quickly through the sixty-six books of the Bible and the thirteen of the Apocrypha, but to do it with a boisterousness that I believe the authors of those books would approve, even if the normally stodgy interpreters you often meet might not!

We will start with a quick overview, then proceed to a quick book-by-book look. We will then try not only to put each book in biblical context, but also to relate it to world history.

Our biblical history, both Old and New Testament, is a very minor part of world history. We in the faith tend to grow up thinking that the Bible and our religious history is somehow the only thing that was happening in the world. But that is not so. As a matter of fact you really have to do some digging to come up with significant stuff about our religious history when you read "non-religious" historians. It's quite a different story when you get past Constantine in 324 A.D. From then on, the Church in the West and in some parts of the Near East was very much (perhaps too much) involved in government. But that is another story.

To get started, it is essential to deal with four principles concerning contents, language, the physical setting,and the social setting of the Bible.

The Contents of the Bible

The principal here is that *HOW YOU INTERPRET A PIECE OF THE BIBLE DEPENDS ON THE TYPE OF WRITING IT IS.*

We all know that when we read poetry we do not expect to meet the precision of fact that we find when you read history. We view a biography differently from the letters of the subject of that biography. That is true in the Bible as well. There are several different types of literary genre here. For instance, the Old Testament contains seventeen historical books, five poetic books, and seventeen prophetic books; while the New Testament contains four biographical books, a historical book, twenty-one letters and tracts, and an apocalyptic book (a writing professing to reveal the future, usually written in highly symbolic language).

On page 177 you will see that the order of listing these books is different in Protestant, Catholic, and Jewish Bibles. Further, in the Jewish tradition, some of what we call "history" is categorized as "former prophets" and "writings."

The Apocrypha ("hidden away") contains three historical books, four moralistic novels, two didactic pieces (fitted for or intended for teaching), a devotional piece, an apocalyptic book, and four prophetic portions.

So far I have listed the books that we will be looking at one by one in this text. But it is important to realize that a number of other books have had acceptance among many Jews and Christians down through the years. Early Christians produced a variety of gospels, histories, epistles, and apocalypses. These writings imitating the Old and New Testament style and content are called "pseudepigrapha" or "spurious works purporting to emanate from biblical characters." That is they have titles or ascriptions which indicate that they were written by some biblical character, but there is no real evidence that convinces scholars that they are, in fact, the real McCoy.

For instance there exist books called: "Adam and Eve," the "Martyrdom of Isaiah," the "Testaments of the Twelve Patriarchs," the "Gospel of Thomas," and the "Gospel of Nichodemus" (also known as the "Acts of Pilate"). In addition, there are epistles of Bartholomew and of the Egyptians, and letters to the Laodicians and to Seneca.

The point here is that we must first understand the type of writing we are reading before we can interpret it properly.

The Language of the Bible

The principal here is that *SINCE NONE OF THE BIBLE WAS*

WRITTEN IN ENGLISH WE NEED TRANSLATIONS, AND ALL TRANSLATIONS ARE INTERPRETATIONS.

Basically, the language of the Old Testament is Hebrew and that of the New Testament is Greek. But in the 3rd century B.C., the Hebrew Old Testament was translated into Greek in Alexandria, Egypt. It was called the Septuagint for the number of elders (seventy) that did the translating.

The early Hebrew of the Old Testament was difficult to read because there was no separation between words, there was no separation between sentences or paragraphs, there were no vowels, and it was all written in what we would call capital letters. Further, there were no chapter or verse indications, for they came much, much later.

Here is an example of how a familiar Old Testament sentence might have looked:

THLRDSMYSHPHRDSHLLNTWNTHMKSMT
LDWNGRNPSTRS

Add vowels, separate the words, and use upper and lower case letters and you get a verse you might have memorized in your youth from Psalm 23:

The Lord is my shepherd, I shall not want; he makes me
to lie down in green pastures.

You can readily see that through the years of copying the various documents by hand, there was plenty of opportunity for error to creep in.

Conjure up in your mind this scene from the Middle Ages. There are no such things as copying machines, not even moveable type. If you want a copy of anything, you do it by hand. If you want multiple copies, you might have someone read the original out loud while several others copy down on parchment what they hear. It is a monastery on a hot August afternoon about 4:00 P.M. The monks are tired, having worked all day at this, and the reader is drowsy. How easy to miss a word, or a sentence, or to confuse one thing for another, or perhaps just put it in your own, more brief words!

Though it sounds somewhat irreverent, let me give you another example of language copying difficulty. When the Hebrews finally added vowels to their language, instead of adding them between the consonants as we do, scribes put them below the line of printing. Vowels were a series of dots called vowel points. They resemble "fly specks." Since the old monasteries were full of flies and manuscripts were laid out on tables for copying purposes, you can well imagine how a few extra vowels (or changed ones) may have gotten in quite by accident.

The Physical Setting

The principle here is that *THERE IS A CORRELATION BE-TWEEN THE WAY PEOPLE THINK, WRITE, ACT, AND LIVE AND THE LAND ON WHICH THEY LIVE.*

The geography of the Bible runs from present day Iraq and Iran in the east to Rome in the west, and from Turkey in the north to Egypt in the south.

Within this region of the globe are at least two ancient cradles of civilization: The Tigris and Euphrates Valley, and the Jordan River rift.

The principle geographic feature that will concern us again and again is called the Fertile Crescent. This stretches from ancient Ur in the east, at the upper end of the Persian Gulf, up in a gentle ark and down through Palestine. All persons moving from one section of this area to another had to follow this crescent, for to the south was an impassable desert.

Another factor to take into consideration is that when you traveled in those days, you took your food with you on the hoof. It was necessary, therefore, to travel where there would be enough grass for cattle, sheep, and goats to graze. We sometimes forget that it was not just Sarah and Abraham who left Ur to walk the 1,000 miles to Palestine; they took along all their household staff and relatives, and a large herd of cattle as well. On the road, they must have looked like the largest Barnum and Bailey Circus parade you could imagine!

Another feature is the very position of the "promised land." Palestine [1] (a word which I will be using despite all the freight that the name now carries) is really a land bridge between two continents; it is bounded on the east by the great Arabian Desert and on the west by the Mediterranean Sea. Up and down this narrow strip of land went a great variety of traders, armies, scholars, and politicians for centuries upon centuries. It was by its very position

---

[1] *Canaan* was probably the earliest name for this area and is used in both biblical and nonbiblical writings. *Israel* was used to refer to the northern part of the land and *Judah* to the southern at the time of the divided kingdom. The use of *Israel* ceased after the fall of the northern kingdom. The Persians called the area *Judah* when it was one of their provinces. This name was used later during the time of the Maccabeean independence for the whole section and kept by the Romans when they took over. *Philistia,* derived from "the land of the Philistines" in the southwest coast was turned by the Greeks into *Palaestina* and used for the entire costal area. After the Bar-Cochba revolt attempt (132-135 A.D.) the Roman emperor simply designated the whole land as *Provincia Syria Palaestina* leading to the most common usage of *Palestine.*

a cosmopolitan strip of land. Persons living there heard about the affairs of the world from those who came through, and from those it sheltered who had reached the end of their personal journey in life.

The center stage of the events described in the Bible is this small strip of land, almost insignificant when viewed on a global basis, called Canaan, the Promised Land, or Palestine. The Bible itself defines it as extending from the city of Dan in the north to Beer-sheba in the south, only 150 miles as the crow flies. But it is really a state of mind, when all is said and done.

The geographic setting is very important to our understanding of the books of the Bible. Moving from west to east across this area, we find:

A COASTAL PLAIN, a thin strip of flat land along the Mediterranean which is unbroken by any effective natural harbor.

A CENTRAL MOUNTAIN RANGE comprised really of high hills, the loftiest of which rises to 3,320 feet. Jerusalem sits on top of this mountain range.

A GREAT CENTRAL RIFT VALLEY that follows a fault line running from the Sea of Galilee, 680 feet below sea level, down the Jordan River to the Dead Sea, 1,290 feet below sea level at its surface.

TRANSJORDAN, another range of mountains parallel to but much lower than the central range, intersected by three "rivers" that are really just valleys most of the time: the Yarmuk, the Jabbok, and the Arnon.

Looking from north to south, the most obvious feature is the Jordan River, which runs from the Sea of Galilee at 680 feet below sea level, to the Dead Sea at 1,290 feet below sea level. The Jordan Valley is only 12 miles wide. It has a tropical climate and during most of the Bible times was the haunt of lions, a very fearful place to venture.

It is only about forty miles from the Mediteranean coast to Jerusalem, but the ascent is from sea level to an elevation of 2,500 feet. Then from Jerusalem to Jericho by the Dead Sea is a drop of about 3,300 feet in fifteen miles.

Thus, the biblical lands are really a small area about 150 miles long and 80 miles wide; it is about the size and shape of the state of Vermont at the latitude of the state of Georgia.

The Social Setting

The principle here is that *PEOPLE   TEND TO PATTERN THEIR   RELIGIOUS   UNDERSTANDING   IN   RELATION   TO THEIR TYPE OF SOCIAL ORGANIZATION.*

During the 2,000 years of history covered by the Bible there is a wide diversity of social settings. Listed in approximate chronological order they are:

NOMADS who wandered rather aimlessly, living in tents.

SHEPHERDS who settled down somewhat, but moved with their animals seeking fresh grazing land.

SLAVES, primarily in Egypt.

WANDERERS who lived during the Exodus time; they made a vast transition, and gained identity and war skills.

WARRIORS who subdued the land and claimed permanent spots to settle.

FARMERS, who now settled "forever." They accommodated themselves to the land and to the rhythm of planting and harvesting.

TRADERS who reached out to far cities to exchange a variety of goods.

This is an amazing spread. In the course of Biblical time,

people moved from family to tribe to city; from a classless to a stratified pattern of life; from patriarchal government to theism to monarchy (though most of the time they were ruled by other nations); and from animism, magic, fetishism, henotheism (a religion that assumes the existence of other gods but holds particular relation to one's own), and finally to monotheism.

A small stage and a short time frame, but immense action!

A Brief Flick Through 2,000 Years of History

It is important at this point to grasp the historical sweep of the whole story of the Bible before we begin our romp through the particular books. You will find that I have devised "historical interludes" from time to time to relate what is happening in the world scene as I tell the story of the particular book or group of books being discussed. But for a few moments I want you to get caught up in the larger picture. This is somewhat like a TV presentation aired during the American Bicentennial when the 200 year history of the United States flashed by in just five minutes;- hold on and watch the map!

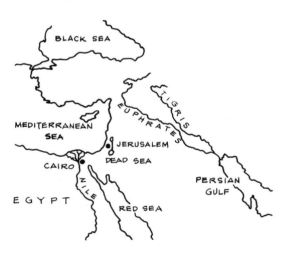

SARAH and ABRAHAM started it all when they left Ur

near the Persian Gulf about 1750 B.C. (the pyramids in Egypt were already about 1,000 years old at this point).

ISAAC and REBEKAH, JACOB and RACHAEL wandered around Palestine with occasional visits to Egypt during drought times (flocks need water at least every other day).

JOSEPH (Jacob and Rachael's son) was sold into slavery and taken to Egypt, where he became a dream interpreter and won promotion to a high state position under the pharaoh.

THE TRIBE came to Egypt for food and stayed to enjoy the better life. But they kept to themselves, not adopting Egyptian customs and thus becoming ghettoized. As "different" people, they were easy to use as scapegoats and eventually became enslaved. (We sometimes miss the point that these people were in Egypt for over 400 years.)

MOSES came on the scene around 1290 B.C. About this time, several mighty powers were breaking up and Egypt lost some of its power, retreating to Egypt proper. This weaker position of a once mighty power opened the way for Moses to challenge the pharaoh and insist that the oppressed people be let go.

A series of important events followed:

PASSOVER occurred, the last straw with the pharaoh in resisting release.

THE EXODUS from Egypt and the receiving of the ten commandments followed. Then spies were sent to see what Palestine was like.

JOSHUA and CALIB reported their findings, and people felt unprepared to do effective battle.

WANDERING IN THE WILDERNESS, these weak former slaves learned to be fighters and to have a vision of what they might become. This was a major identity change.

MOSES DIED ON MOUNT NEBO just before they entered
the "promised land."

JOSHUA took over as supreme military commander after
Moses' death, and, crossing the Jordan from east to west
near Jericho, began a brilliant operation to secure the
land and settle the tribes. At this point they were a
confederacy.

JUDGES administered the law, though many of them were
more like local warlords (Gideon, Sampson, Deborah, and
others). They settled disputes within and between tribes
and continued a mopping up operation to keep the land.

FARMING BECAME MUCH MORE IMPORTANT, and
people began settling into a pattern quite different from
wandering. They therefore adopted both a new life style
and a new code of ethics in another significant identity
change.

SAMUEL had to deal with the demand of the people for a
king "like everyone else has." He tried to dissuade them
by saying Yahweh alone was king, but he finally gave in.

SAMUEL ANNOINTED SAUL as the first king. Saul was
a very uptight, fearful, cautious, person who even suc-
cumbed to calling upon "spirits" to help him out of a jam.

DAVID became king in about 1000 B.C., after becoming
Saul's champion by slaying Goliath In an astute political
move designed to unite the tribes, David selected as his
capital an obscure city, not important to any of the
tribes, and then brought the Ark of the Covenant there to
also make it the center of worship.

SOLOMON, the fruit of David's well-known relationship
with Bathsheba, succeeded him as king. Solomon constructed a permanent building to house the Ark (after
seeing to his own need of luxury), and engaged in

widespread trade that brought great riches and renown to the small state.

THE KINGDOM DIVIDED in 922 B.C. when Solomon's successor botched the administration of the realm. From that point on, the north was called ISRAEL and the south JUDAH. Ten tribes lived in Israel and two in Judah.

PROPHETS like Amos, Hosea, and Micah kept warning the people that their immoral behavior and their failure properly to worship and serve Yahweh would endanger their future.

ISRAEL FELL TO THE ASSYRIANS in 722 B.C., despite the warnings of the prophets.

JOSIAH tried to hold out for independence for Judah, instituting a political and religious reform, but Judah fell to Babylon in 587 B.C.

THE EXILE is the period when the best of the citizens were taken as captives to Babylon (near the place from which Sarah and Abraham came). There they lived from 587 to 538 B.C. until Cyrus, a Persian, overthrew the Babylonians to become king.

THE RETURN of the Jews to Jerusalem happened over a number of years, principally under the leadership of Ezra and Nehemiah.   This was the time of Pericles and Socrates in Greece.

ALEXANDER THE GREAT made the world Greek in the 4th century B.C., only to die at the age of thirty-three in 323 B.C. in Babylon. His generals carved up his empire and one of them, Antiochus IV, made a determined effort to make the Jews accept Greek culture.

THE MACCABEAN REVOLT in 167 B.C. was the re-sponse to that effort. Under Judas Mattathias, the Jews won independence   for a few years until they were crushed by the Romans; Pompey marched into Jerusalem in 63 B.C.

JESUS was born in about 4 B.C. and the Crucifixion and Resurrection occurred about 30 A.D.

PAUL toured the Mediterranean area, arriving in Rome about 65 A.D.

THE FALL OF JERUSALEM in 70 A.D. at the hands of Titus, later to become Caesar, brought an end to a brief Jewish revolt; Masada held out until 73 A.D.

THE BAR COCHBA REVOLT was crushed in 132 A.D. after three years of bloody fighting.

ISRAEL would not be independent again until 1948.

Part I

The Old Testament

Chapter 1

Old Testament History

Throughout this book I stress the importance of knowing the type of writing with which we are dealing.

We begin our romp by looking at the historical books of the Old Testament, and history simply cannot be read and understood in the same way as poetry. History is written as it is perceived from the point of view of one person, or as one person finally sets down the remembrances of a group of persons, with his own perspective either consciously omitted or unconsciously included. Modern historians attempt to make their writing truly objective. There are, of course, some "personal" histories, where an individual deliberately sets out to say what history has meant to him or her. For example, William Manchester wrote a book titled *The Glory and the Dream,* which he subtitled *A Narrative History of America, 1932-1972,* and Theodore White's book, *In Search of History,* was subtitled, *A Personal Adventure.*

Each human being is unique, and therefore one person's perspective on history is different from another's. In early history a self-centered angle was almost always present, so it is necessary to use the best collaborative tools we have to reconstruct and imagine what those early historians were really trying to say.

There is another factor to consider when we read biblical history; those who wrote, gathered or edited it, truly believed it. This is in striking contrast to writers like Herodotus who wrote in a preface to his *History* (ca. 450 B.C.):

> For myself, my duty is to report all that is said; but I am not obliged to believe it all alike--a remark which may be understood to apply to my whole History.

We are fortunate that we have Herodotus and a few other ancients who traveled through the geographical area discussed in the Bible, for from them we can get some collaboration of biblical stories.

So, as we begin, be fully aware that the writing in the first books of the Bible is a subjective history, believed by those who spoke it. They rehearsed it by their campfires and finally wrote it down for all to remember.

The historical books of the Old Testament include the Pentateuch, a set of early historical records, the records of story tellers and editors, and later histories. We will consider them each in turn.

The Pentateuch

The first sixteen books of the Old Testament describe the origin, unification, defeat, captivity, and restoration of the Hebrew tribes. The first five books comprise the Pentateuch, known also as "The Five Books of Moses" and "The Law." Earliest among the works of the Old Testament, the Pentateuch originally appeared as a scroll almost 50 feet long, but the Greeks, for convenience, divided it into five rolls. The Pentateuch, almost always referred to as "The Law," was the first part of scripture to be canonized, or made official (see page 173). It remains the central document of the Jewish religion, and it occupies a hallowed place in all synagogues.

How many centuries of oral tradition, that is of the telling of the contents by word of mouth around the campfire and at stated assemblies, preceded the actual writing of the Pentateuch we cannot say. But almost five centuries elapsed between its inception and its completion in about 400 B.C. Many persons, unknown by name but diverse in interest and point of view, contributed to the Pentateuch. Scholars have divided the multiple authorship into four major catagories called J, E, D, and P on the basis of stylistic differences between them. We will examine those differences in a moment, but in order to do so we need to look at some very early historical writings.

Early Historical Records

Much of the Pentateuch was part of an oral tradition for centuries before being written down, but the first historical accounts written down soon after the recorded events occurred date from about 1,000 B.C. Stories about Samuel, Saul, and David were composed by their contemporaries, and we know from II Samuel that

David had both a secretary and a recorder. The main characteristic of these early historical accounts is their vividness. Told in a lean style, they give the sense of immediate vitality. They are straight-forward and comparatively free from miraculous explanations of events. Here is an example:

> Saul sent messengers to Jesse, saying, "Send me David your son who is with the sheep." Jesse took five loaves, a skin of wine, and a kid, and sent them to Saul by David his son. And so David came to Saul and entered his service; Saul loved him greatly and David became his armor bearer. Then Saul sent to Jesse saying, "Let David enter my service; he has won my favor." And whenever the spirit from God troubled Saul, David took the harp and played; then Saul grew calm, and recovered, and the evil spirit left him. [1]

Or this lean telling of a very poignant turn in their relationship:

> On their way back, as David was returning after killing the Philistines, the women came out to meet King Saul from all the towns of Israel, singing and dancing to the sound of tambourine and lyre and cries of joy; and as they danced the women sang "Saul has killed his thou-sands, and David his tens of thousands." Saul was very angry; the incident was not to his liking. "They have given David the tens of thousands," he said, "but me only the thousands; he has all but the kingship now." And Saul turned a jealous eye on David from that day forward.[2]

---

[1] I Samuel 16:19-23.

[2] I Samuel 18:6-9.

Storytellers and Editors

Several centuries later, when the kingdom was divided into north and south, a remarkable person in the Southern Kingdom, with a great gift for writing, began to set down the earliest stories from the oral tradition of the people. These were stories preserved over the centuries by persons who knew how to tell or to repeat very accurately stories that they had heard. At this time in history human beings were blessed with this gift; we seem to have lost it since the coming of inexpensive printing, perhaps because we simply do not have to remember anymore. We can "go look it up". But then people were able to remember accurately and retell precisely what they had heard. It is an experience we often have with our children. We read a bedtime story to a child and, being tired, try to skip some sentences. "You skipped a line," they say, even though they cannot read. They remember.

So, in about 850 B.C., beginning with the story of creation found in Genesis 2:4b, some writer began to set down the stories in writing for the first time. They are vivid, dramatic, and full of conversation and human interest. They include such events as the expulsion of Adam and Eve from the garden, the story of Cain and Able, the doom of Sodom, the leading of Moses, Joshua's capture of Jericho, and so on.

A good example of this writer's ability is found in the story of the announcement that ninety-year-old Sarah would have a baby. Listen to the dialogue:

> Yahweh appeared [to Abraham] at the Oak of Mamre while he was sitting by the entrance of the tent during the hottest part of the day. He looked up, and there he saw three men standing nearby. As soon as he saw them he ran from the entrance of the tent to meet them, and bowed to the ground. My lord, he said, "I beg you, if I find favor with you, kindly do not pass your servant by. A little water shall be brought; you shall wash your feet and lie down under the tree. Let me fetch a little bread and you shall refresh yourselves before going further."
>
> Abraham hastened to the tent to find Sarah. "Hurry," he said, "kneed three bushels of flour and make loaves." Then, running to the cattle, Abraham took a fine calf and

gave it to the servant, who hurried to prepare it. Then, taking cream, milk, and the calf he had prepared, he laid all before them, and they ate while he remained standing near them under the tree.

"Where is your wife Sarah?" they asked him. "She is in the tent," he replied. Then his guest said, "I shall visit you again next year without fail, and your wife will then have a son." Sarah was listening at the entrance of the tent behind him. Now, Abraham and Sarah were old, well on in years, and Sarah had ceased to have her monthly periods. So Sarah laughed to herself, thinking, "Now that I am past the age of childbearing, and my husband is an old man, is pleasure to come my way again?" But Yahweh asked Abraham, "Why did Sarah laugh and say, 'Am I really going to have a child now that I am old?' Is anything too wonderful for yahweh? At the same time next year I shall visit you again and Sarah will have a son." "I did not laugh," Sarah said, lying because she was afraid. But he replied, "Oh yes, you did laugh." [3]

This particular storyteller, who wrote in about 850 B.C., is called "J" by scholars because his word for God was YHWH, earlier translated as Jehovah, and because the setting of most of his stories was Judah.

A second phase of writing these stories began about a century later. Another skilled writer set down the same stories in language more smooth, less forceful. There is also less use of direct dialogue between persons and Yahweh, as in the example just cited of Abraham, Sarah, and Yahweh.

Scholars have identified these parts of the Pentateuch and have called the author "E" because he used the term Elohim for God, and because they were written from the point of view of the northern tribes, one of which was Ephriam.

An typical example of this writing may be seen in the story of the finding of Moses in the reeds by the river in Egypt. But one of my favorites is the near sacrifice of Isaac. Note that the conversa-

---

[3] Genesis 18:1-15.

tion with Yahweh is sparse, official, not easy, and that it is clear
that Yahweh is not seen, only heard.

It happened some time later that God put Abraham to
the test. "Abraham, Abraham," he called. "Here I am,"
he replied. "Take your son," God said, "your only child
Isaac, whom you love, and go to the land of Moriah.
There you shall offer him as a burnt offering, on a
mountain I will point out to you."

Rising early next morning, Abraham saddled his ass and
took with him two of his servants and his son Isaac. He
chopped wood for the burnt offering and started on his
journey to the place God had pointed out to him. On the
third day Abraham looked up and saw the place in the
distance. Then Abraham said to his servants, "Stay here
with the donkey. The boy and I will go over there; we
will worship and come back to you."

Abraham took the wood for the burnt offering, loaded
it on Isaac, and carried in his own hands the fire and the
knife. Then the two of them set out together. Isaac
spoke to his father Abraham. "Father," he said. "Yes, my
son," he replied. "Look," he said "here are the fire and
the wood, but where is the lamb for the burnt offering?"
Abraham answered, "My son, God himself will provide the
lamb for the burnt offering." Then the two of them went
on together.

When they arrived at the place God had pointed out to
him, Abraham built an altar there, and arranged the
wood. Then he bound his son Isaac and put him on the
altar on top of the wood. Abraham stretched out his
hand and seized the knife to kill his son.

But the angel of Yahweh called to him from heaven.
"Abraham, Abraham," he said. "I am here," he replied.
"Do not raise your hand against the boy," the angel said.
"Do not harm him, for now I know you fear God. You
have not refused me your son, your only son." Then
looking up, Abraham saw a ram caught by its horns in a
bush. Abraham took the ram and offered it as a burnt
offering in place of his son.

The angel of Yahweh said " . . . because you have
done this, because you have not refused me your son,

> your only son, I will shower blessings on you. I will
> make your descendants as many as the stars of heaven
> and the grains of sand on the seashore. . . . [4]

Now that is storytelling!

Well, war and calamity produce various types of heroes and we
can be glad that some literary hero rescued "E's" documents when
the Northern Kingdom fell to the Assyrians in 722 B.C. That person
brought them south to safety, where some editor cut apart both "J's"
document and "E's" and integrated them. That is why you sometimes
get the same story told twice, usually one right after the other.

But the integrating or interweaving was far from over. In 621
B.C., a king by the name of Josiah led a successful (if brief) revolt
against the Assyrians to throw off the "puppet" state mentality and
clear away the pagan religious rites that had come with it. He was
a conservative who wanted to return the nation to the law of
Moses. He ordered the temple repaired and in the process someone
found the book we now call Deuteronomy.

One wonders if it was "planted," for it conveniently provided
the theological basis for Josiah's revolution. It was sober in style
and laid a great deal of focus on the legal aspects of morality.
(More on this revolution on page 51.) It was obviously not the first
law code, so it was called the "second law," or Deuteronomy. Its
message is summarized in this famous passage:

> And now, Israel, what does Yahweh your God ask of
> you? Only this: to fear Yahweh your God, to follow all
> his ways, to love him, to serve Yahweh your God with all
> your heart and all your soul, to keep the commandments
> and laws of Yahweh that for your good I lay down for
> you today. [5]

Jesus quotes this, and all the Jewish world of his day and ours
quotes the verse in 6:4, called the Shema:

---

[4] Genesis 22:1-17.

[5] Deuteronomy 10:12-13.

Listen, Israel: Yahweh our God is the one Yahweh. You shall love Yahweh your God with all your heart, with all your soul, with all your strength. Let these words I urge on you today be written on your heart. You shall repeat them to your children and say them over to them whether at rest in your house or walking abroad, at your   lying down or at your rising. . . . [6]

When I taught, and would tell my students that I was going to deal with Deuteronomy, they often groaned and complained about a "dry, dusty old law book." But that meant that they had never taken the time to read it. Deuteronomy has many of the most sensitive passages in the whole of the Old Testament. One of my favorite chapters is 24, and here are some verses:

If a man is newly married, he shall not join the army nor is he to be pestered at home; he shall be left at home free of all obligations for one year to bring joy to the wife he has taken.

If anyone is found kidnapping one of his brothers, one of the sons of Israel, whether he makes him his slave or sells him, that thief must die. You must banish this evil from your midst.

If you are making your fellow a loan on pledge, you are not to go into his house and seize the pledge, whatever it may be. You must stay outside, and the man to whom you are making the loan shall bring the pledge out to you. And you must return it to him at sunset so that he can sleep in his cloak and bless you; and it will be a good action on your part in the sight of Yahweh your God.

You are not to exploit the hired servant who is poor and destitute, whether he is one of your brothers or a stranger who lives in your towns. You must pay him his wage each day, not allowing the sun to set before you do, for he is poor and is anxious for it; otherwise he may appeal to Yahweh against you, and it would be a sin for you.

---

[6] Deuteronomy 6:4-7.

When reaping the harvest in your field, if you have overlooked a sheaf in that field, do not go back for it. Leave it for the stranger, the orphan and the widow, so that Yahweh your God may bless you in all your undertakings.

When you beat your olive trees, you must not go over the branches twice. Let anything left be for the stranger, the orphan and the widow.

When you harvest your vineyard, you must not pick it over a second time. Let anything left be for the stranger, the orphan and the widow.

Remember that you were a slave in the land of Egypt. This is why I lay this charge on you. [7]

At this point we have "J", "E", and "D" all put together, but there is one other piece to be fitted in before we have the Pentateuch.

Much later, perhaps around 500 B.C., after the people had returned from exile and rebuilt the temple and much of Jerusalem, a group of priests took their turn at telling the stories of the people from their point of view. By this time in history they were directing the religious life of the people and were in charge of the temple. They were naturally concerned about ritualistic observances and liturgy. Their contributions to the Old Testament are not terribly inspiring, except for a few sections such as the hymn of creation with which Genesis begins:

In the beginning God created the heavens and the earth. Now the earth was a formless void, there was darkness over the deep, and God's spirit hovered over the water. God said, "Let there be light. . . ." [8]

The priests probably reordered the whole of the history recorded by "J" and "E" into four large epochs, each corresponding to a special rite or ritual which was central to them as priests and their function; the four epochs are:

---

[7] Deuteronomy 24:5, 7, 10-15, 19-22.

[8] Genesis 1:1-3.

FROM THE CREATION TO THE FLOOD, with the Sabbath and its observance as a climax;

FROM THE FLOOD TO ABRAHAM, with the prohibition against eating anything with blood in it (the dietary laws) as the central ritual focus;

FROM ABRAHAM TO MOSES, with the rite of circumcision as the ritual climax; and

THE EPOCH OF MOSES, with passover as the ritual focus.

The priests seem to have been interested in giving a rationale for the rituals of the people and especially for their own part in organizing the religious life in the temple.

With the integration of the "P" (for priestly) material, the Pentateuch as we know it was complete, comprising the books of Genesis, Exodus, Leviticus, Numbers, and Deuteronomy.

Deuteronomic History

When Josiah "found" the book of Deuteronomy in 621 B.C., other writings were also discovered. These writings had probably existed for centuries as part of an oral tradition, and some parts may have been written down even before this date, but they all surfaced at this time.

Joshua

The book of Joshua is the history of the conquest, allotment, and occupation of the Promised Land. It is integrally related to the first five books we have looked at and is often thought of as a part of them. For this reason the group of six books is sometimes referred to as the Hexateuch.

In the call of Moses and the beginning of the Exodus recorded in the book of Exodus, Yahweh not only frees the people from slavery in Egypt, but also gives them "the home of the Canaanites, the Hittites, the Amorites, the Perizzites, the Hivites, and the Jebusites." There follows the wilderness wanderings, and, some years later, we find Moses dead and Joshua leading an invasion of Canaan.

We often forget that Canaan was not vacant land at the time; in fact, it was well populated and the Canaanites took a dim view of this Yahweh who had given "his people" the moral go-ahead to take the land away from them by force. Thus, the book of Joshua contains the story of a holy war concluding with two speeches by Joshua to his people. The speeches can be summarized as follows:

> So now, fear Yahweh and serve him perfectly and sincerely; put away the gods that your ancestors served beyond the River and in Egypt, and serve Yahweh. But if you will not serve Yahweh, choose today whom you wish to serve, whether the gods that your ancestors served beyond the River, or the gods of the Amorites in whose land you are now living. As for me and my House, we will serve Yahweh. [9]

Judges

The book of Judges follows much the same style and story as the book of Joshua. After Joshua's conquest, a series of local warlords kept order among the people of their particular tribes and between the tribes of Israel. They were also able to gather warriors to beat back the remnants of other nations who had formerly controlled the land.

The book begins with a direct hookup to Joshua:

> Then Joshua told the people to go, and the Israelites went away, each to his own possession, to occupy the land. . . . [10]

---

[9] Joshua 24:14-15.

[10] Judges 2:6.

It then proceeds to tell the stories of individual judges like Deborah (neat to have a woman identified in this strong position so early in the history of the faith, but don't forget how strong Miriam was during the Exodus!), Gideon, Sampson, and others. The people probably originally referred to them as "saviors."

The song of Deborah in Chapter 5 is considered one of the most ancient substantial pieces of literature in the Old Testament.

I and II Samuel, I and II Kings

Originally, these four books were one single work entitled "Concerning the Kingdoms." They contain narratives that are masterpieces of the oriental storyteller's art.

The career of Samuel is described at the very beginning of this history, but the main theme here is the kingship of Israel and especially of the big three: SAUL, DAVID, and SOLOMON. The rest of the kings in both the north and the south are discussed in much less detail, and the account primarily shows how the conduct of Saul, David, and Solomon shaped the affairs of both state and religion.

A brief outline of these four books will give a quick overview of the contents:

I Samuel, 1-25 The story of Samuel.
              9-31 The story of Saul.
          16-31 The story of David.

II Samuel, 1-24 The story of David, continued.

I Kings, 1-11 The story of Solomon.

I Kings, 11-II Kings 17 The story of both kingdoms.

II Kings, 18-25 The story of Judah.

We also find in these books some unique historical gems. Only here, for instance, do we hear the story of the Ark (I Samuel 4-6), the history of the rise of Saul (I Samuel 9-14), the saga of David's rise (I Samuel 16), and the story of the succession to David's throne (II Samuel 9-20).

David is my favorite Old Testament figure. He is more often quoted and referred to in the Judaic/Christian tradition than any other person except Jesus, and these books center on him.

Here is the story of a man who births a nation. But it is also the story of a person who came to grips with a great tension; David lived with a sense of the sovereignty of God, yet knew that this God had placed in the hands of ordinary mortals the power of decision for self and society. David lives a new theology here. He made mistakes, but he made them boldly and so advanced not only the nation of Israel but also a mature concept of the faith.

If I were to pick one episode to show David's strength, it would be when he helped to bring the Ark of the Covenant to Jerusalem for placement in the temple:

> They placed the Ark of God on a new cart . . . Uzzah walked alongside the Ark and Ahio went in front. David and all the House of Israel danced before Yahweh with all their might, singing to the accompaniment of lyres, harps, tambourines, castanets, and cymbals. Thus David and all the House of Israel brought up the Ark [to Jerusalem] with acclaim and the sound of the horn. Now as the ark of Yahweh entered the Citadel of David, Michal [David's wife] was watching from the window and saw King David leaping and dancing before Yahweh; and she despised him in her heart. . . . As David was coming back to bless his household, Michal . . . went out to meet him. "What a fine reputation the king of Israel has won himself today," she said, "displaying himself under the eyes of his ser-vant-maids, as any buffoon might display himself." David answered Michal, "I was dancing for Yahweh, not for them. As Yahweh lives . . . I shall dance before him and demean myself even more. In your eyes I may be base, but by the maids you speak of I shall be held in honor. [11]

---

[11] II Samuel 6:3-22.

Later History

The books in this category, I & II Chronicles, Ezra, and Nehemiah, were written much later than those we have considered. In 587 B.C. the Southern Kingdom of Judah was defeated by the Babylonians, and the decision-makers, the ruling class, businessmen, and craftspersons were taken into exile. Under a new Persian government, ushered in by the successful campaign of Cyrus, the people were released and permitted to return to Jerusalem to rebuild the temple and the city. This took place over a long time and under various leaders. It was during this time that I and II Chronicles and the books of Ezra and Nehemiah were written.

I and II Chronicles

These books retell the stories of I & II Samuel and I & II Kings from a priestly perspective. They are much concerned with genealogy and morality, and there is a great interest in the temple and in the work of and rationale for the priests.

In the Jewish Bible these books, along with the books of Ezra and Nehemiah, are grouped with "The Writings" rather than in the historical setting. They clearly represent pious reflections on earlier accounts.

Ezra and Nehemiah

These books originally were one. They give a history of the people for almost a hundred years, from the first return of the exiles to the end of Nehemiah's leadership. They tell of the rebuilding of the temple and of the successive returns of the exiles from Babylon.

These two books are our only direct sources for that period, and they are therefore very important to our understanding of the development of our faith and its history.

Chapter 2

Prophecy

A Definition Interlude

All the groups of people we know something about, even the earliest and most primitive, have had a "prophetic office" in their structure of life. Such an office was necessary, for they believed in gods and spirits who controlled their destiny, and they needed a way to communicate with them. Generally they set aside certain people who were considered gifted, persons who had access to the thoughts of the gods. These persons were endowed with cultic power to interpret the mind of the gods and to communicate it to the tribe or nation.

In the simplest terms, the difference between the prophets outside Israel and those of Israel was that those outside Israel were FOREtellers, who divined the future via omens in nature, such as the particular flight pattern of birds or the examination of entrails, or through dreams and trances, while those inside Israel were primarily FORTHtellers, speaking fearlessly the mind of Yahweh. They were not so much interested in telling what the future would be as in telling people what Yahweh thought of their actions and lives.

The very word "prophet" comes from two Greek words, *pro* meaning "for," and *phetes* meaning "speaker." A prophet was thus one who spoke for another, specifically one who spoke for Yahweh, and in the New Testament the following verse supports that definition,

For it was not through any human whim that men proph-

esied of old; men they were, but, impelled by the Holy
Spirit, they spoke the words of God. [12]

Yahweh spoke to these prophets just like he speaks to men and
women today who listen for the "still small voice" within. The
communication is not by words out of the sky, but by messages
given directly to minds and hearts.

A good many historians are pessimistic about the prophets of
the Bible. They point out that they spoke and wrote Hebrew, and
the language died (it was revived as a living language only about
1950); they urged reform, but their world did not want reforming;
they analyzed politics, but the politicians were too engrossed to
care; and they promoted religion, but the people preferred sin.

Perhaps the worst thing that has happened to the words of
these truly remarkable persons is that there have been too many
who have wanted to make fortune-tellers out of them.

Early Prophets

Obviously, from the definition above, not all the prophets of
the Old Testament wrote their message or had it written for them.
Early in the history of the people of Israel there were those who
"spoke for" but did not write. Moses is a prime example. Listen to
this neat exchange between Yahweh and the reluctant Moses:

> Moses said to Yahweh, "But, my Lord, never in my life
> have I been a man of eloquence, either before or since
> you have spoken to your servant. I am a slow speaker
> and not able to speak well."
> "Who gave man his mouth?" Yahweh answered him.
> "Who makes him dumb or deaf, gives him sight or leaves
> him blind? Is it not I, Yahweh? Now go, I shall help
> you to speak and tell you what to say."
> "If it please you, my Lord," Moses replied "send anyone
> you will!" At this, the anger of Yahweh blazed out
> against Moses, and he said to him, "There is your brother

---

[12] II Peter 1:21.

Aaron, is there not. I know that he is a good speaker. Here he comes to meet you. When he sees you, his heart will be full of joy. You will speak to him and tell him what message to give. I shall help you to speak, and him too, and instruct you what to do. He himself is to speak to the people in your place; he will be your mouthpiece, and you will be as the god inspiring him. And take this staff into your hand; with this you will perform the signs. [13]

And Moses did speak for Yahweh, as did Samuel and Nathan and a host of others who do not have "prophetic books" assigned to them in the Bible.

But I especially want to single out two persons who are truly non-writing prophets by trade.

Elijah

Eligah's story is told beginning with I Kings 17. He fearlessly speaks a word of censure against King Ahab for having erected an altar to the pagan god Baal. A great drought comes upon the land and sets the scene for a classic confrontation between this one fearless man speaking for Yahweh and the four hundred "prophets" of Baal

Ahab says to Elijah:

"So there you are, you scourge of Israel!" [Kings don't like it when prophets disagree with them.] And Elijah answers, "Not I . . . I am not the scourge of Israel, you and your family are; because you have deserted Yahweh and gone after the Baals." [14]

At any rate, they have a contest on Mt. Carmel, which is a beautiful setting, a high promontory jutting out into the sea. Both Elijah and the four hundred prophets of Baal put a bull on an altar

---

[13] Exodus 4:10-17.

[14] I Kings 18:17-18.

with lots of wood underneath. The Baalists go first, calling on Baal
to send fire to light the wood and consume the offering. They
cried out, they danced, they did everything imaginable, but no fire.
    Then it was Elijah's turn. To heighten the drama, Elijah had
the whole thing drenched with water, not just once, but three times,
until the water ran off the wood and filled a trench around the
altar.

> Then the fire of Yahweh fell and consumed the holocaust
> and wood and licked up the water in the trench. When
> all the people saw this they fell on their faces. "Yahweh
> is God," they cried, "Yahweh is God." Elijah said, "Seize
> the prophets of Baal; do not let one of them escape."
> They seized them and Elijah took them down to the wadi
> Kishon, and he slaughtered them there. [15]

Now that is speaking fearlessly for Yahweh!
    Later prophets were to identify Elijah as the one to announce
the coming of the Messiah. To this day, Jews set an extra place at
the table each time they observe the Passover, and even open the
door to the house to see if Elijah is standing outside.
    We need also to remember that Jesus was called Elijah and that
Elijah was one of the figures that appeared on the Mount of
Transfiguration with Jesus. (See Mark 9:4.)

Elisha

    Elisha was well-to-do; after all, he was plowing with twelve
oxen when Elijah called him to drop it all and come with him. He,
too, became a national figure and took part in the political affairs
of the nation, before anyone thought that the church should not
have anything to do with politics.
    His story begins with I Kings 19:19.

---

[15] I Kings 18:38-40.

Seven Great Writing Prophets

Four of these, Amos, Hosea, I Isaiah, and Micah, lived and wrote during the 8th century B.C. What a mighty time that was. Karl Jaspers called this an "axil period" of history. It was one of those rare times when significant things were happening all over the world. From Cornwall to China there was a new thrust in the history of humans:

> IN CORNWALL, tin mines produced materials for the improved shapes of weapons, tools, and utensils of Europe's Bronze Age.

> IN GREECE, Homer was writing the *Iliad* and the *Odyssey,* and Iona was a cultural center.

> IN ASSYRIA, this was a time of unprecedented expansion and cultural advance; Zoroaster was a mighty figure writing and teaching.

> IN INDIA, the sacred Hindu scriptures, *The Upanishads,* were being written.

> IN CHINA, Laotse was writing and teaching, laying the foundation for Taoism.

And in the midst of all this, at the very crossroads, lay Israel and Judah.

In this small land between the continents, Amos, Hosea, I Isaiah, and Micah watched, perceived, and spoke their words for Yahweh.

Amos

Amos was a herdsman from the village of Tekoa on the harsh slopes of the eastern side of the central mountain range, down toward the Dead Sea. This layman had fire in his belly. His message was like his life, austere and uncompromising. He had a social conscience before anyone thought of the word. On behalf of Yahweh he spoke out for justice for the poor.

This was a time of affluence, prosperity, and peace in Israel, and Amos details the luxury. They had winter AND summer homes, silk upholstery, ivory objects d'art, and high grade meat, wine, and oil, but they didn't give a damn about the poor.

Amos wrote and spoke about 750 B.C. He lived in the Southern Kingdom of Judah, but he delivered his message in the north. He gathered an audience and began to speak of the sins and evils of the nations around about the Northern Kingdom. Thus he quickly got their ear and sympathy, then paused dramatically and said:

> For the three crimes, the four crimes, of Israel, I have made my decree and will not relent:
> Because they have sold the virtuous man for silver and the poor man for a pair of sandals;
> Because they trample on the heads of ordinary people and push the poor out of their path;
> Because father and son have both resorted to the same girl, profaning my holy name;
> Because they stretch themselves out by the side of every altar on clothes acquired as pledges, and drink the wine of the people they have fined. [16]

Or again, hear this layman level his charge that the people who were once slaves themselves, who were once themselves outcasts in Egypt and the very bottom of the heap, that these people had now forgotten in a time of prosperity what it was to be poor:

> Listen to this, you who trample on the needy and try to suppress the poor people of the country, you who say, "When will New Moon be over so that we can sell our corn, and sabbath, so we can market our wheat?" Then by lowering the bushel, raising the shekel, by swindling and tampering with the scales, we can buy up the poor for money, and the needy for a pair of sandals, and get a price even for the sweepings of the wheat. [17]

---

[16] Amos 2:6-8.

[17] Amos 8:4-6.

His message is that Yahweh will not forget what they have done to the poor!   Yahweh is not interested in the fact that they have ritualistically gone to temple Sabbath after Sabbath,   Yahweh is interested in righteousness and shalom.

> I hate and despise your feasts, I take no pleasure in your solemn festivals.   When you offer me holocausts, I reject your oblations, and refuse to look at your sacrifices of fattened cattle.   Let me have no more of the din of your chanting, no more of your strumming on harps.   But let justice flow like water, and integrity like an unfailing stream. [18]

Hosea

In many ways Hosea is the other side of the coin from Amos. He spoke and wrote at about the same time, 740 B.C., and lived and did his work in the north, in Israel.   He was a sensitive, tender person who felt with passion the unfaithfulness and corruption of Israel.   Here is an example:

> When Israel was a child I loved him, and I called my son out of Egypt.   But the more I called to them, the further they went from me; they have offered sacrifice to the Baals and set their offerings smoking before the idols.   I myself taught Ephraim to walk, I took them in my arms; yet they have not understood that I was the one looking after them.   I led them with reins of kindness, with leading-strings of love.   I was like someone who lifts an infant close against his cheek; stooping down to him I gave him his food. [19]

Hosea saw and spoke to the same Israel as Amos, but he had a different perspective.   The oppression of the poor by the rich did

---

[18] Amos 5:21-24.

[19] Hosea 11:1-4.

not escape him, but he was more concerned with the general disregard of moral obligations, wholesale lying, murder and stealing, than with the problems of the poor.

> Sons of Israel, listen to the word of Yahweh, for Yahweh indicts the inhabitants of the country: there is no fidelity, no tenderness, no knowledge of God in the country, only perjury and lies, slaughter, theft, adultery and violence, murder after murder. [20]

And above all, he gave us, for the first time, a clear understanding of Yahweh as a God of love. He did this by using the illustration of a husband deeply in love with his wife. He showed how that husband would go after his wayward wife even when she had become a prostitute to bring her back with no recrimination. Yahweh, he said, is like that!

A Quick Comparison of Amos and Hosea

Amos and Hosea shared a strong concept of monotheism (belief in one god), a powerful sense of righteousness over ritual, and the idea that calamities were a sign of Yahweh's displeasure.
Neither is mentioned anywhere else in the Old Testament. All we know of each of them is from their own books.
Hosea did not have the international outlook of Amos, and he did not possess the passionate demand for social justice that Amos had. But Hosea went beyond Amos in expressing that the relationship between Yahweh and the people was one of love and forgiveness.
So here in these first two literary prophets we find the establishment of two of the great themes of the Judaic/Christian tradition: Amos declaring the impartial justice of Yahweh, and Hosea teaching the unalterable love of Yahweh.

---

[20] Hosea 4:1-2.

I Isaiah (Chapters 1-39)

I Isaiah is truly one of the giants of the Old Testament. His message combines both the justice of Amos and the mercy of Hosea. In verses 11-18, Isaiah says:

> What are your endless sacrifices to me? says Yahweh.
> I am sick of holocausts of rams
> and the fat of calves.
> The blood of bulls and of goats revolts me.
> When you come to present yourselves before me,
> who asked you to trample over my courts?
> Bring me your worthless offerings no more,
> the smoke of them fills me with disgust. . . .
> Take your wrong-doing out of my sight.
> Cease to do evil.
> Learn to do good,
> search for justice,
> help the oppressed,
> be just to the orphan,
> plead for the widow.
>
> Come now, let us talk this over,
> says Yahweh.
> Though your sins are like scarlet,
> they shall be as white as snow;
> though they are red as crimson,
> they shall be like wool.

Isaiah did his work about 740 B.C. and we know that he was a city person and a resident of Jerusalem. He had a shrewd knowledge of the great powers. Where Amos and Hosea warned of the coming of Assyria, Isaiah actually saw the Assyrians come and take over the Northern Kingdom. Isaiah was an aristocrat; he dealt with the king face-to-face and had access to the court. He was more poetic in his writing; he did not blurt out the truth, it came out in imaginative language.

Unlike Amos and Hosea, Isaiah's writing covers a whole lifetime, from youth to old age, with all the precipitous changes that took place in his own thinking. He saw and experienced the independence of Judah give way to Assyrian vassalage. He saw and experienced the destruction of Israel and Syria by Assyria. He was probably over sixty years of age when he died.

His main message can be summarized this way:

> The human is nothing before God.
> God is passionately ethical.
> God's interest is centered in Jerusalem.
> God demands repentance and faith.
> Only a remnant will be saved.
> There will be a glorious future for the remnant.
> A messiah will come to restore the glory of Israel.

In two passages (Isaiah 9:1-7 and 11:1-5) he introduces the concept of a wonderful king who will bring about a new order:

> The people that walked in darkness
> has seen a great light;
> on those who live in a land of deep shadow
> a light has shown.
> You have made their gladness greater,
> you have made their joy increase;
> they rejoice in your presence
> as men rejoice at harvest time,
> as men are happy when they are dividing the spoils.
>
> For the yoke that was weighing on him,
> the bar across his shoulders,
> the rod of his oppressor,
> these you break as on the day of Midian.
>
> For all the footgear of battle,
> every cloak rolled in blood,
> is burnt, and consumed by fire.
>
> For there is a child born for us,
> a son given to us
> and dominion is laid on his shoulders;
> and this is the name they will give him:
> Wonder-Counsellor, Mighty-God,
> Eternal-Father, Prince-of-Peace.

Wide is his dominion in a peace that has no end,
for the throne of David
and for his royal power,
which he establishes and made secure
in justice and integrity.
From this time onwards and for ever,
the jealous love of Yahweh Sabaoth will do this.

Listen again as Isaiah gives us yet another poetic description
of the messiah to be:

A shoot springs from the stock of Jesse,
a scion thrusts from his roots:
on him the spirit of Yahweh rests,
a spirit of wisdom and insight,
a spirit of counsel and power,
a spirit of knowledge and of the fear of Yahweh. . . .

He does not judge by appearances,
he gives no verdict on hearsay,
but judges the wretched with integrity,
and with equity gives a verdict for the poor of the
        land.
His word is a rod that strikes the ruthless,
his sentences bring death to the wicked.

Integrity is the loincloth round his waist,
faithfulness the belt about his hips.

Then this vision of the peaceable kingdom:

The wolf lives with the lamb,
the panther lies down with the kid,
calf and lion cub feed together
with a little boy to lead them.
The cow and the bear make friends,
their young lie down together.
The lion eats straw like the ox.

The infant plays over the cobra's hole;
into the viper's lair
the young child puts his hand.
They do no hurt, no harm,
on all my holy mountain,
for the country is filled with the knowledge
    of Yahweh
as the waters swell the sea. [21]

Four themes have their first appearance here:

The holiness of God found in 6:3 and the familiar "holy, holy, holy is Yahweh Sabaoth."

Jerusalem is seen as the focus of Yahweh's love.

The doctrine of the remnant, which tended to break up the solidarity of the nation, which led to the individualism of Ezekiel, and which projected a pessimistic concept of the future of humankind as a "while many are called, few are chosen" theme.

The figure of the Messiah which fired the imaginations of generations afterward, which reappeared in various writings, and which gave the New Testament church its inspiration for its faith in Jesus.

So Isaiah, an urban citizen of Jerusalem writing in about 740 B.C., gave us forever a set of brilliant word pictures, ringing challenges, and inexorable demands, including a vision of the holiness of God, a scorn of all foul things, a championing of the poor, a vision of the messianic age to be, all clustered into thirty-nine chapters!

With these first three writing prophets, we have the three mighty themes of the nature of Yahweh: Isaiah, holiness; Amos, justice; Hosea, love.

---

[21] Isaiah 11:1-9.

Micah

Like Amos, Micah was a country person, but unlike Amos, he came not from the desert, but from a green and fertile village area on the opposite side of the mountain. His daily scene was of grazing cattle, wheat fields, and olive groves. We know that he lived and wrote around 710 B.C. Micah spoke for the poor and as one of them. He was horrified at the luxurious and degenerate life of the city (any city, but especially, Jerusalem), and he realized that he and his fellow peasants were paying for it. Though he was not a political revolutionary or agitator, still he wanted justice between humans and a right attitude toward Yahweh.

Micah spoke out against the abuse of power by judges, the prevalence of bribery, the exploitation of the poor and needy by rich landowners, and the lust for money.

He was red hot with righteous indignation. Against the tyranny of the rich. he said:

Woe to those who plot evil,
who lie in bed planning mischief!
No sooner is it dawn than they do it
--their hands have the strength for it.
Seizing the fields that they covet,
they take over houses as well,
owner and house they confiscate together,
taking both man and inheritance.
So Yahweh says this:
Now it is I who plot
such mischief against this breed
as your necks will not escape;
nor will you be able to walk proudly,
so evil will the time be. [22]

Against the rulers who oppress the people, he said:

Then I said:
Listen now, you princes of the House of Jacob,
rulers of the House of Israel.

---

[22] Micah 2:1-3.

Are you not the ones who should know what is right,
you, enemies of good and friends of evil?
When they have devoured the flesh of my people
and torn off their skin
and crushed their bones;
when they have shredded them like flesh in a pot
and like meat in a cauldron,
then they will cry out to Yahweh.
But he will not answer them.
He will hide his face at that time
because of all the crimes they have
committed. [23]

But there is a promise of peace and universalism:

He will wield authority over many peoples
and arbitrate for mighty nations;
they will hammer their swords into plowshares,
their spears into sickles.
Nation will not lift sword against nation,
there will be no more training for war.
Each man will sit under his vine and his fig
        tree,
with no one to trouble him.
The mouth of Yahweh Sabaoth has spoken it. [24]

And finally, this classic verse for righteousness over ritual:

With what gift shall I come into Yahweh's
        presence
and bow down before God on high?
Shall I come with holocausts,
with calves one year old?
Will he be pleased with rams by the thousand,
with libations of oil in torrents?

---

[23] Micah 3:1-4.

[24] Micah 4:3-4.

Must I give my first-born for what I have done wrong,
the fruit of my body for my own sin?
--What is good has been explained to you, man;
this is what Yahweh asks of you:
only this, to act justly,
to love tenderly
and to walk humbly with your God. [25]

An Historical Interlude

Assyria finally succeeded in conquering Egypt in 650 B.C. under Ashurbanapal. Earlier, Sennacherib had conquered much of Israel, coming to the very gates of Jerusalem.

Manasseh was king in Judah at this time and revolt broke out all over the sprawling Assyrian empire, in Babylon, in Egypt, and in the north, as the Scythians and Meads attacked from there.

But Manasseh followed an expedient policy of remaining, at least officially, an obedient vassal state. So while Assyrian armies moved through Israel to Egypt to quell revolt, Judah was left virtually unmolested. Manasseh's policy had other costs, of course; patriotic Judeans were unhappy with Manasseh's kowtowing to a foreign king. Furthermore, he gave official sanction to astrology, magic, and human sacrifice, so that paganism was not only permitted but actively sponsored by Manasseh.

This stirred again the deep prophetic roots of the people of Yahweh. Many rediscovered Moses and the covenant from the days of the wilderness wanderings.

Menasseh died in 642 B.C. and his son Amon tried to continue his father's relations with Assyria. But Amon was murdered after only two years on the throne during a patriotic revolt.

Thus Josiah came to be king at the age of eight.

Ashurbanapal died in about 633 B.C. and a sense of Assyria's weakness flashed across the empire and again excited people to revolt. Josiah was secure enough after seven years to seize the moment for some radical change.

The prophet Zephaniah comes in here.

---

[25] Micah 6:6-8.

Zephaniah

Zephaniah was an aristocrat who traced his heritage back with pride; he had an understanding of world history and had been given a good education. He was not a poet, but a flaming evangelist. His book comes through as a call to repentance. In many ways his teaching is an echo of Amos from a century before.

Zephanian expresses Yahweh's judgment on alien gods, court officials, merchants, unbelievers, and others:

On the day of Yahweh's sacrifice,
I will punish the ministers,
the royal princes,
and all those who dress themselves
in foreign style.
On that day I mean to punish
all those who are near the throne,
those who fill the palace of their lord
with violence and deceit. . . .

When that time comes
I will search Jerusalem by torchlight,
and punish the men
who are stagnating on their lees,
those who say in their hearts,
"Yahweh has no power
for good or for evil."
Then their wealth will be given up to looting,
their households to plundering.
They built houses, did they? They will not live in them.
They planted vineyards, did they? They will not drink their
    wine.
The great day of Yahweh is near,
near, and coming with all speed.
How bitter the sound of the day of Yahweh,
the day when the warrior shouts his cry of war.
A day of wrath, that day,
a day of distress and agony,
a day of ruin and of devastation,
a day of darkness and gloom,
a day of cloud and blackness,
a day of trumpet blast and battle cry
against fortified town
and high corner-tower.
I am going to bring such distress on men
that they will grope like the blind
(because they have sinned against Yahweh);
their blood will be scattered like dust,
their corpses like dung.
Neither their silver nor their gold
will have any power to save them. [26]

Again the remnant will survive the anger of Yahweh when he
will, "sweep away everything off the face of the earth".

In your midst I will leave
a humble and lowly people,

---

[26] Zephaniah 1:8-9, 12-18.

and those who are left in Israel will seek
   refuge in the name of Yahweh.
They will do no wrong,
will tell no lies;
and the perjured tongue will no longer
be found in their mouths.
But they will be able to graze and rest
with no one to disturb them. [27]

Most scholars believe that the Zephaniah prophecy was one of the preludes to the revival in Judah called Josiah's reform. Remember (see page 21) that this was the time when the Book of Deuteronomy was "found" in the temple. The context was not so much "repairs of the temple" as it was a cleansing from the temple of all remnants of Assyrian influence. This was a national revolt. It was 621 B.C.

Two other "minor" prophets wrote during this period of Josiah's reform and just afterward: Nahum and Habakkuk. Jeremiah also lived during this period; his prophecy dates ca. 626-586 B.C.

Josiah was a very simplistic conservative, and his revival was an attempt to turn things back to the "good old days," with no accounting for the complexities of either the present or the future. His interpretation of the simple "moral logic" of Deuteronomy put a great strain on the people and led, eventually, to a period of disillusionment.

Nahum

Assyria was finally defeated in 612 B.C. under the combined assault of the Babylonians, the Meads, and the Scythians. Nahum gives vent to the pentup frustration, anger, and hatred of the people.

Originally this was probably an acrostic poem. Each line began with a succeeding character of the Hebrew alphabet. But we can no longer see its form because it has become disordered.

Yahweh is a jealous and a vengeful God,

---

[27] Zephaniah 3:12-13.

Yahweh avenges, he is full of wrath;
Yahweh takes vengeance on his foes,
he stores up fury for his enemies.
Yahweh is slow to anger but immense in power.
Most surely Yahweh will not leave the guilty unpunished. [28]

Listen to this piece of hate poetry:

Woe to the city soaked in blood, full of lies,
stuffed with booty,
whose plunderings know no end!
The crack of the whip!
The rumble of wheels!
Galloping horse,
jolting chariot,
charging cavalry,
flash of swords,
gleam of spears. . .
a mass of wounded,
hosts of dead,
countless corpses;
they stumble over the dead.
So much for all the whore's debauchery,
for that wonderful beauty, for that cunning
    witch
who enslaved nations by her debauchery
and tribes by her spells.
I am here! Look to yourself! It is Yahweh
    Sabaoth who speaks.
I mean to lift your skirts as high as your face
and show your nakedness to nations,
your shame to kingdoms.
I am going to pelt you with filth,
shame you, make you a public show.
And all who look on you
will turn their backs on you and say,
"Nineveh is a ruin."

---

[28] Nahum 1:2.

Could anyone pity her?
Where can I find anyone to comfort her? [29]

Historical Interlude

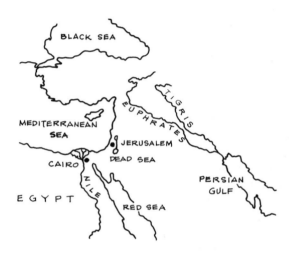

At this time, Assyria is collapsing, and the Egyptian Pharaoh Necho unexpectedly and belatedly comes on strong to "rescue" Assyria, on the logic that a weak Assyria is better than a strong Babylon. As the Egyptians march through Judah, they are cut off at the pass of Megiddo by Josiah, who, remember, would have been only too glad to get rid of Assyria. Though Josiah is defeated and executed and Necho's army marches clear to the Euphrates, the Egyptians are defeated in the famous battle at Carchemish by the Babylonians under Nebuchadnezzar. After the battle, the Egyptians are literally chased back across the fertile crescent to the very borders of Egypt.

---

[29] Nahum 3:1-7.

Babylon is now ruler of the world and Nebuchadnezzar is king of the hill.

This really shakes the Israelites, who had hoped "Good King Josiah" and his reform movement would bring them national independence. Instead, they find themselves vassals of Babylon and just as bad off as they were under Assyria, and the new administration in Jerusalem reverts to appeasement and tolerance of paganism and syncritism.

This elicits a cry of anguish from Habakkuk.

Habakkuk

Habakkuk was a prominent citizen of Jerusalem, a "free thinker" who raised doubts concerning the simplistic concept of Yahweh's direction of history. In that vein he writes:

> I will stand on my watchtower,
> and take up my post on my battlements,
> watching to see what he will say to me,
> what answer he will make to my complaints.
> Then Yahweh answered and said,
> "Write the vision down,
> inscribe it on tablets
> to be easily read,
> since this vision is for its own time only:
> eager for its own fulfillment, it does not
>   deceive;
> if it comes slowly, wait,
> for come it will, without fail.
> See how he flags, he whose soul is not at
>   rights,
> but the upright man will live by his faithfulness. [31]

Habakkuk helps us to see that Yahweh does not stifle a sincere questioner, that complex problems of history cannot have direct, simplistic answers, and that in dealing with doubt, it's OK to take your time and wait expectantly.

---

[31] Habakkuk 2:1-4.

Also in this book is that old Sunday School opening verse:

The Lord is in his holy temple,
let all the earth be silent before him. [32]

Jeremiah

Jeremiah also lived in the midst of crisis. As we mentioned above, Manassah was king-vassal to Assyria and permitted all sorts of pagan practices. Assyria was being attacked, and "Good" King Josiah seized the moment to clear the temple and revolt, but he was defeated and killed. Babylon took over Assyria's empire and Nebuchadnezzar conquered Jerusalem.

In the midst of all this, Jeremiah lived and spoke. His life and work spaned almost fifty years, and we know a good deal about him, for he had a secretary by the name of Baruch.

Jeremiah came from a suburb of Jerusalem and was well educated. He was a sophisticated rebel whose sharp wit and words were directed against dimwitted kings, princes, diplomats, and false prophets. He was a lonely figure, mostly unpopular during his prophetic years, for he was "against the whole land." His commission from yahweh was told this way:

Then Yahweh put out his hand and touched my
    mouth and said to me:
"There! I am putting my words into your
    mouth.
Look, today I am setting you
over nations and over kingdoms,
to tear up and to knock down,
to destroy and to overthrow,
to build and to plant." [33]

Anyone daring to speak like this is bound to get his, and Jeremiah did, more than once. A memorable experience is found in this passage:

---

[32] Habakkuk 2:20.

[33] Jeremiah 1:9-10.

But Shephatiah son of Mattan, Gedaliah son of Pashhur, Jucal son of Shelemiah, and Pashhur son of Malachiah heard the words which Jeremiah was saying to all the people. "Yahweh says this, 'Anyone who stays in this city will die by sword, famine, or plague; but anyone who leaves it and surrenders to the Chaldeans will live; he will escape with his life'. Yahweh says this: 'This city will certainly be delivered into the power of the army of the king of Babylon, who will capture it.'"

These leading men accordingly spoke to the king. "Let this man be put to death: he is unquestionably disheartening the remaining soldiers in the city, and all the people too, by talking like this. The fellow does not have the welfare of this people at heart so much as its ruin." "He is in your hands as you know," King Zedekiah answered, "for the king is powerless against you." So they took Jeremiah and threw him into the well of Prince Malachiah in the Court of the Guard, letting him down with ropes. There was no water in the well, only mud, and into the mud Jeremiah sank. [34]

Jeremiah was saved this time by a palace eunuch.

Even though he foretold Jerusalem's destruction at the hands of the Babylonians (and then saw it happen), he never gave up hope for restoration. In a memorable event, when Jerusalem was under seige and Jeremiah under house arrest, he sent for his cousin and arranged to buy a piece of property. His purchase will have no value in Babylonian hands, but Jeremiah sees the day when Jerusalem will be restored! That's confidence buying par excellence! [35]

Thus, Jeremiah taught the sovereignty and majesty of Yahweh in the midst of changing times. His speeches were packed with energy, and he walked about with a yoke chaffing his neck, wearing special clothes, and smashing pots and bottles to illustrate his message.

Finally, a new covenant is announced:

---

[34] Jeremiah 38:1-6.

[35] See Jeremiah 32:9-15.

> See, the days are coming--it is Yahweh who speaks--when
> I will make a new covenant with the House of Israel (and
> the House of Judah), but not a covenant like the one I
> made with their ancestors on the day I took them by the
> hand to bring them out of the land of Egypt. They broke
> that covenant of mine, so I had to show them who was
> master. It is Yahweh who speaks. No, this is the
> covenant I will make with the House of Israel when those
> days arrive--it is Yahweh who speaks. Deep within them
> I will plant my Law, writing it on their hearts. Then I
> will be their God and they shall be my people. There will
> be no further need for neighbor to try to teach neighbor,
> or brother to say to brother, "Learn to know Yahweh!"
> No, they will all know me, the least no less than the
> greatest--it is Yahweh who speaks--since I will forgive
> their iniquity and never call their sin to mind. [36]

There will be an exile, but in 32:37-41 he says there will also be a
return:

> I mean to gather them from all the countries where I
> have driven them in my anger, my fury, and great wrath.
> I will bring them back to this place and make them live
> in safety. Then they shall be my people, and I will be
> their God. I will give them a different heart and
> different behavior so that they will always fear me, for
> the good of themselves and their children after them. I
> will make an everlasting covenant with them; I will not
> cease in my efforts for their good, and I will put respect
> for me into their hearts, so that they turn from me no
> more. It will be my pleasure to bring about their good,
> and I will plant them firmly in this land, with all my
> heart and soul.

These and other strong passages are used in the Jewish community
all over the world today in connection with the return to present-

---

[36] Jeremiah 31:31-34.

day Israel and the hope to dwell in security on that particular piece
of land.

Historical Interlude

Like the Exodus which freed the people from slavery in Egypt
and set them on the long course of self-identification, so the Exile
proved to be another watershed in this discovery of who they were
to be.

Nebuchadnezzar, the Babylonian king, following the custom of
the day, deported the first-class citizens of Jerusalem (the leaders,
rulers, artisans) back to his own capital. There he thought he could
keep an eye on them, prevent rebellion back home in Jerusalem, and
also be enriched by their creativity, while still getting the produce
of the conquered land from the peasants who were still there tilling
the land.

Jeremiah refused to go! He stayed behind after the first
deportation. Ezekiel did go, and became the prophetic leader of the
people "by the waters of Babylon." More of this later.

The few leaders left in Judah soon got rambunctious and tried to rebel. Many of them left for Egypt just before the Babylonian army came down on them, and they took unwilling Jeremiah with them. This series of events is called the "diaspora," the scattering of the Jews. It is important to realize that the diaspora was not a single event. For many years Jews had been going abroad, for example as traders and government officials under David and Solomon, so that by the time of the divided kingdom there were already significant numbers of Jews in various major cities beyond Israel. Some were also dispersed by the Assyrians when they conquered the Northern Kingdom.

Egypt became one of the major centers of Judiasm, as we shall see later in connection with the translation of the Hebrew scriptures. But the main story of the "people of Yahweh" continues through the Jews in exile in Babylon.

There, torn away from their beloved land and temple, a new concept appeared. Worship was possible in a foreign land. This set the scene for the development of the synagogue, a worshipping community in every town and place.

Experiencing this double dislocation, from land and temple, was Ezekiel.

Ezekiel

Was Exekiel a troubled psychotic, or only a prophet with bizarre illustrations? Both views have been supported by a wide variety of scholars. We do know he was of the upper class of Jerusalem, influenced by the witness of Jeremiah, and probably a participant in Josiah's reform.

His writing is filled with vivid images, weird visions, and strange creatures:

> I looked; a stormy wind blew from the north, a great cloud with light around it, a fire from which flashes of lightning darted, and in the center a sheen like bronze at the heart of the fire. In the center I saw what seemed four animals. They looked like this. They were of human form. Each had four faces, each had four wings. Their legs were straight; they had hooves like oxen, glittering

like polished brass. Human hands showed under their wings; the faces of all four were turned to the four quarters. Their wings touched each other; they did not turn as they moved; each one went straight forward. As to what they looked like, they had human faces, and all four had a lion's face to the right, and all four had a bull's face to the left, and all four had an eagle's face. Their wings were spread upwards; each had two wings that touched, and two wings that covered his body; and they all went straight forward; they went where the spirit urged them; they did not run as they moved. [37]

Ezekiel also speaks of cherubs and chariots of fire (chapter 10), and of a valley full of dry bones (chapter 37). But, as with other prophets, the hope was there:

I, Yahweh, have spoken. I shall make a covenant of peace with them; I shall rid the country of wild animals. They will be able to live safely in the wilderness and go to sleep in the woods. I shall settle them round my hill; I shall send rain at the proper time; it will be a fertile rain. The trees of the countryside will yield their fruit and the earth its produce; they will feel safe on their own farms. And men will learn that I am Yahweh when I break their yokestraps and release them from their captors. No more will they be a prey to foreign countries, no more will they be eaten by wild animals in this country. They will live without fear and no one will disturb them again. I shall make splendid vegetation grow for them; no more will they suffer from famine in this land; no more will they have to bear the insults of other nations. And men will learn that I, their God, am with them and that they, the House of Israel, are my people--it is the Lord Yahweh who speaks. And you, my sheep, are the flock I shall pasture, and I am your God--it is the Lord Yahweh who speaks. [38]

---

[37] Ezekiel 1:4-12.

[38] Jeremiah 34:24-31.

II Isaiah   (Chapters 40-66 of Isaiah)

The superb writing in these chapters was added to the book of Isaiah, but it is clearly of a different style and written by a different author. We actually know nothing about the author beyond the facts that the chapters were written in Babylon during the exile and the style indicates that they were written by a person of culture and education.

> Who was it measured the water of the sea
>   in the hollow of his hand
> and calculated the dimensions of the heavens,
> gauged the whole earth to the bushel,
> weighed the mountains in scales,
> the hills in a balance? [39]

The book from which this passage comes is called the "Consolation of Israel," and from beginning to end it is a cry of good news!   "Comfort ye, comfort ye my people," he began, just as dramatically as Handel many centuries later set it in his "Messiah." It is a collection of poems, each reflecting hope. The captives are given promises of great things that would come to pass. Little wonder that Mark and others in New Testament times would latch onto the words "good news; the kingdom of God is at hand!"

Furthermore this prophet takes up, makes clear, and expands the "universal" strain of the Old Testament. Yahweh is not just the personal possession of Israel, but the God of all persons everywhere.

> I, Yahweh, have called you to serve the cause
>   of right;
> I have taken you by the hand and formed you;
> I have appointed you as covenant of the people
>   and light of the nations,
> to open the eyes of the blind,
> to free captives from prison,

---

[39] Isaiah 40:12.

and those who live in darkness from the
dungeon. [40]

And see also this scene of the appearance of all the nations before
the creator:

Assemble, come, gather together,
survivors of the nations.
They are ignorant, those who carry about
their idol of wood,
those who pray to a god
that cannot save.
Speak up, present your case,
consult with each other.
Who foretold this
and revealed it in the past?
Am I not Yahweh?
There is no other god besides me,
a God of integrity and a savior;
there is none apart from me.
Turn to me and be saved,
all the ends of the earth,
for I am God unrivalled. [41]

Israel itself, as a people, are to be Yahweh's servant to bring
this good news to all people. God speaks to them as a whole saying
that the covenant made with their ancestors required them to be
servants of all, that they were "chosen" or "called" not for special
privilege, but for special service.

A case can also be made that this prophet was telling of a
special person, a prophet to come, like Moses, to deliver and to
lead. This writer gives us four poems describing the "servant" that
is to come; all four are powerfully written, but the fourth is the
greatest of them all, some of the finest writing the world has
known.

---

[40] Isaiah 42:6-7.

[41] Isaiah 45:20-22.

1.   Here is my servant whom I uphold,
      my chosen one in whom my soul delights.
      I have endowed him with my spirit
      that he may bring true justice to the nations.

      He does not cry out or shout aloud,
      or make his voice heard in the streets.
      He does not break the crushed reed,
      nor quench the wavering flame. [42]

2.   Islands, listen to me,
      pay attention, remotest peoples
      Yahweh called me before I was born,
      from my mother's womb he pronounced my
            name.

      He made my mouth a sharp sword,
      and hid me in the shadow of his hand.
      He made me into a sharpened arrow,
      and concealed me in his quiver.

      He said to me, "You are my servant (Israel)
      in whom I shall be glorified;"
      while I was thinking, "I have toiled in vain,
      I have exhausted myself for nothing;"

      and all the while my cause was with Yahweh,
      my reward with my God.
      I was honored in the eyes of Yahweh,
      my God was my strength.

      And now Yahweh has spoken,
      he who formed me in the womb to be his
            servant,
      to bring Jacob back to him,
      to gather Israel to him:

---

[42] Isaiah 42:1-3.

It is not enough for you to be my servant,
to restore the tribes of Jacob and bring back
    the survivors of Israel;
I will make you a light of the nations
so that my salvation may reach to the ends of
    the earth. [43]

3.   The Lord Yahweh has given me
a disciples tongue.
So that I may know how to reply to the
    wearied
he provides me with speech.
Each morning he wakes me to hear,
to listen like a disciple.
The Lord Yahweh has opened my ear.

For my part, I made no resistance,
neither did I turn away.
I offered my back to those who struck me,
my cheeks to those who tore at my beard;
I did not cover my face
against insult and spittle.

The Lord Yahweh comes to my help,
so that I am untouched by the insults.
So, too, I set my face like flint;
I know I shall not be shamed.

My vindicator is here at hand. Does anyone
    start proceedings against me?
Then let us go to court together.
Who thinks he has a case against me?
Let him approach me.

The Lord Yahweh is coming to my help,
who dare condemn me?

----

[43] Isaiah 49:1-6.

They shall all go to pieces like a garment
devoured by moths. [44]

4.   See, my servant will prosper,
        he shall be lifted up, exalted, rise to great
            heights.

        As crowds were appalled on seeing him
        --so disfigured did he look
        that he seemed no longer human--
        so will the crowds be astonished at him,
        and kings stand speechless before him;
        for they shall see something never told
        and witness something never heard before:
        Who could believed what we have heard,
        and to whom has the power of Yahweh been
            revealed?
        Like a sapling he grew up in front of us,
        like a root in arid ground.
        Without beauty, without majesty (we saw him),
        no looks to attract our eyes;
        a thing despised and rejected by men,
        a man of sorrows and familiar with suffering,
        a man to make people screen their faces;
        he was despised and we took no account of
            him.

        And yet ours were the sufferings he bore,
        ours the sorrows he carried.
        But we, we thought of him as someone
            punished,
        struck by God, and brought low.
        Yet he was pierced through for our faults,
        crushed for our sins.
        On him lies a punishment that brings us peace,
        and through his wounds we are healed.

        _____

[44] Isaiah 50:4-9.

We had all gone astray like sheep,
each taking his own way,
and Yahweh burdened him
with the sins of all of us.
harshly dealt with, he bore it humbly,
he never opened his mouth,
like a lamb that is led to the slaughterhouse,
like a sheep that is dumb before its shearers
never opening its mouth.

By force and by law he was taken;
would anyone plead his cause?
Yes, he was torn away from the land of the
      living;
for our faults struck down in death.
They gave him a grave with the wicked,
a tomb with the rich,
though he had done no wrong
and there had been no perjury in his mouth.

Yahweh has been pleased to crush him with
      suffering.
If he offers his life in atonement,
he shall see his heirs, he shall have a long life
and through him what Yahweh wishes will be
      done.

His soul's anguish over
he shall see the light and be content.
By his sufferings shall my servant justify many,
taking their faults on himself.

Hence I will grant whole hordes for his tribute,
he shall divide the spoil with the mighty,
for surrendering himself to death
and letting himself be taken for a sinner,

while he was bearing the faults of many
and praying all the time for sinners. [45]

These magnificent poems were loved by the people for their
beauty, depth, and truth as they dealt with the age old question of
suffering and servanthood. The people did not think of them as a
prediction of the Messiah; rather, they understood them as speaking
to their own calling, as a whole people, to be the "suffering
servant." Over 500 years later they were read and reread by a
young Jew who became the embodiment of the suffering servant.

The Later Prophets

The "later" prophets acted and wrote during and after the
return of the people from exile. During this time, the fertile
crescent, including Palestine, was under the rule of Semites from the
time of Abraham and Sarah on; Old Babylon, at the time of
Hammurabi and Abraham, gave way to Assyria at the time of Amos
and Hosea, which in turn gave way to the Neo-Babylonians (called
Chaldeans in the Bible), who lasted only through the reign of
Nebuchadnezzar.

This was the time when Judah was in exile.

During this period in the north, the Meads and Persians began
to push south. In 550 B.C. King Cyrus of Persia defeated the
Meads and took over Lydia from Croesus, and then, in 539 B.C.,
took over Babylon. Cyrus' "enlightened" administration gave permis-
sion for the Jews to return to Jerusalem. The Persian Empire lasted
for about 200 years until Alexander the Great did it in.

---

[45] Isaiah 52:13-53:12.

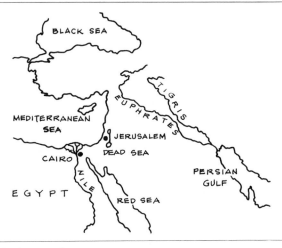

Now, on with the prophets.

Haggai

The people of Israel ostensibly went back to Jerusalem to rebuild the temple. Instead, after only a quick effort at the temple, they went about rebuilding their houses and businesses, walls and orchards.

Haggai came on the scene to challenge the people to resume the rebuilding of the temple. He was probably an older person, for he asks "Who is there left among you that saw this temple in its former glory? And how does it look to you now? Does it seem nothing to you?" [46] He had been with the people in exile, and had come back with the original first return but somewhat later.

In four brief homilies couched in everyday language, he addressed the people as Yahweh's spokesman.

Then along came a sidekick who picked up Haggai's words and put some fire in them. Both of them were preaching in Jerusalem in the same year, 520-519 B.C. What a billing!

---

[46] Haggai 2:3.

Zechariah

Zechariah was born during the exile. He was a sensitive, young, and energetic man. He chided, but did not threaten, and encouraged the people to get on with the rebuilding of the temple.

It is interesting to contrast him with Amos and others who saw too much "temple worship" and not enough social action. While there is no evidence of social concern among these returned exiles, neither is there much evidence of ritual.

Zechariah speaks of two themes of the prophetic tradition. He pictured Jerusalem remaining "unwalled because of the great number of men and cattle there will be in her," symbolic of the return of all exiles no matter where they were:

> Yahweh Sabaoth says this.
> I am coming back to Zion
> and shall dwell in the middle of Jerusalem.
> Jerusalem will be called Faithful City
> and the mountain of Yahweh Sabaoth, the
>   Holy Mountain.

> Yahweh Sabaoth says this.
> Old men and old women will again sit
>   down
> in the squares of Jerusalem:
> every one of them staff in hand
> because of their great age.
> And the squares of the city will be full
> of boys and girls
> playing in the squares.

> Now I am going to save my people
> from the countries of the East
> and from the countries of the West.
> I will bring them back
> to live inside Jerusalem.
> They shall be my people

and I will be their God
in faithfulness and integrity. [47]

Zechariah also speaks of the Messiah:

Rejoice heart and soul, daughter of Zion!
Shout with gladness, daughter of
        Jerusalem!
See now, your king comes to you;
he is victorious, he is triumphant,
humble and riding on a donkey,
on a colt, the foal of a donkey.
he will banish chariots from Ephraim
and horses from Jerusalem;
the bow of war will be banished.
He will proclaim peace for the nations.
His empire shall stretch from sea to sea,
from the River to the ends of the earth. [48]

There are other verses scattered in Zechariah that have been
used by the Christian church as part of the proof of Jesus' being
the Messiah:

And they weighed out my wages:
thirty shekels of silver.
But Yahweh told me,
"Throw it into the treasury,
this princely sum
at which they have valued me."
Taking the thirty shekels of silver,
I threw them into the Temple of Yahweh
into the treasury. [49]

---

[47] Zechariah 8:3-5,7,8.

[48] Zechariah 9:9-10.

[49] Zechariah 11:13.

They will look on the one
whom they have pierced;
they will mourn for him
as for an only son,
and weep for him
as people weep
for a first-born child. [50]

These I received in the house of my friends.
Awake, sword, against my shepherd
and against the man who is my
    companion--
it is Yahweh Sabaoth who speaks.
I am going to strike the shepherd
so that the sheep my be scattered. . . . [51]

Historical Interlude

Well, someone or something got the Jews going, perhaps over the guilt of living in rather "luxurious panelled houses" while the house of Yahweh lay still in ruins. Certainly the Samaritans and the Syrians did not help with all their harassment. But the temple was rebuilt and rededicated by 515 B. C. It is called now the "second temple." There is a neat footnote here that reminds us that not much is new, for it is recorded that when some of the older ones who had known Solomon's temple saw the new one, "they wept with a loud voice." Someone had made some changes!

We get a glimpse of what life was like from this time until the arrival of Nehemiah in 445 B.C. through the brief words of two or three truly "minor" prophets. I have put them all here because we know that they spoke and wrote after the dedication of the temple, though some put Joel much later. None of them is all that great.

---

[50] Zechariah 12:10.

[51] Zechariah 13:6-7.

Obadiah

The Book of Obadiah is the shortest in the Old Testament. Called by George Adam Smith, "an indignant oration," it has only one theme; according to Obadian, the Edomites, who seized part of the territory of Judah after the fall of Jerusalem, are going to get their due.

The Edomites were the descendants of Esau (remember, Jacob traded some stew for Esau's inheritance), and lived south of the Dead Sea. They had good land and had made out quite well. In typical sibling feuding they refused to let Moses pass through their territory during the Exodus, and in Joshua's battle for the Promised Land they fought against him.

Judas Maccabeus drove them out of Southern Judah in 164 B.C. during the Maccabean revolt that led to independence. Then John Hyracanus forced them to accept Judaism, but they became the hated Idumeans of the New Testament times and gave the Jews the Herod family!

At any rate, Obadiah comes on like a Fourth of July orator and denounces the Edomites as godless sinners facing complete destruction. The followers of John the Baptist and Jesus might have appreciated it if that had happened, but it didn't.

Malachi

We don't know much about Malachi, though we sense that things were not going well for the people as a whole at the time he lived. There was a lot of complaining going on when he spoke and wrote.

Malachi accused the people of not taking their religion seriously, and especially of not paying their tithes to the temple. And so we have here a good stewardship text:

> Can a man cheat God? Yet you are cheating me. You ask, "How are we cheating you?" In the matter of tithes and dues. The curse lies on you because you, yes you the whole nation, are cheating me. Bring the full tithes and dues to the storehouse so that there may be food in my house, and then see if I do not open the floodgates of

heaven for you and pour out blessing for you in abund-
ance. [52]

Joel

A plague of locusts was devouring the crops at the time Joel
wrote. We have no idea when this took place, but Joel tells the
people this plague is the result of their sinfulness. He urges them
to repent. The seventy-three verses of this book describe the
devastation of the land by the locusts as a sign of judgment, a call
to repentance, and a promise of relief and of a future glory.

There are a lot of mean words and phrases in Joel that TV
preachers love to take out of context and use to frighten people.

_____

[52] Malachi 3:8-10.

Chapter 3

Poetry

The classical definition of poetry is "imaginative writing; the representation, often the idealized representation, of nature or history, especially in verse." We view poetry quite differently from writing that purports to be history, for instance, even though the poetry may speak about historical events.

The people of the ancient world appreciated poetry, and fine examples can be found in the old cultures of the various nations surrounding the Jews and among the Greeks and Chinese. The distinguishing mark of Old Testament poetry is not rhyme or meter so much as parallelism. Sometimes this is a repeating of an idea or thought or statement in different words:

> The Law of Yahweh is perfect,
>   new life for the soul;
> The decree of Yahweh is trustworthy,
>   wisdom for the simple. [53]

Sometimes it is contrasting one line or thought with the next:

> A mild answer turns away wrath,
>   sharp words stir up anger.
> The tongue of wise men distills knowledge,
>   the mouth of fools spews folly. [54]

There are distinctly poetic books in the Bible, and there are also many poetic passages integrated into the historical books.

---

[53] Psalms 19:7.

[54] Proverbs 15:1-2.

Early Folk Songs

The Song of Moses and Miriam

Moses demanded of the Pharaoh in Egypt, "Let my people go," and the Exodus from slavery began. The first real barrier and test the escapees faced was the Red Sea. The people marched out, faced this obstacle, and panicked. But Moses urged them on, saying, "Yahweh will provide." And the sea was opened and they crossed as on dry ground. But the Egyptians came after them. Capture was imminent. But Moses stretched out his arms and Yahweh stopped the wind. The waves closed over the pursuing Egyptians.

It is in this context that Moses and Miriam sing a song. It begins by announcing that it is a song, and it undoubtedly became the "freedom now" marching song of the wilderness wanderers. Then Moses and the sons of Israel sang this song in honor of Yahweh:

Yahweh I sing: he has covered himself in glory,
horse and rider he has thrown into the sea.
Yah is my strength, my song,
he is my salvation.
This is my God, I praise him;
the God of my father, I extol him.
Yahweh is a warrior;
Yahweh is his name.
The chariots and the army of Pharaoh he has
        hurled into the sea;
the pick of his horsemen lie drowned in the Sea
        of Reeds.
The depths have closed over them;
they have sunk to the bottom like a stone.
Your right hand, Yahweh, shows majestic in
        power,
your right hand, Yahweh, shatters the enemy.
So great your splendor, you crush your
        foes;
you unleash your fury, and it devours them like
        stubble.

A blast from your nostrils and the waters piled
    high;
the waves stood upright like a dyke;
in the heart of the sea the deeps came
    together. [55]

And on it goes for another ten verses.

Songs in the Wilderness

    As the people of Yahweh moved about in the Sinai Peninsula for those long years, they composed songs in appreciation of the goodness of Yahweh (when they were not complaining, that is).

For the well.
Sing out for the well
that was sunk by the princes
and dug by the leaders of the people
with the scepter, with their staves. [56]

Or when they conquered the first towns of the Promised Land:

Courage, Heshbon!
Well built and well founded,
city of Sihon!
For a fire came out of Heshbon,
a flame from the city of Sihon,
it devoured Ar of Moab,
it engulfed the heights of the Arnon.
Woe to you, Moab!
You are lost, people of Chemosh!
He has turned his sons into fugitives,
his daughters into captives
for Sihon, king of the Amorites.

---

[55] Exodus 15:1-8.

[56] Numbers 21:17-18.

Heshbon has destroyed
the little children as far as Dibon,
the women as far as Nophah,
the men as far as Medeba. [57]

The Song of Deborah

This is a long song, taking thirty-one verses. It begins:

They sang a song that day, Deborah and
    Barak . . . and the words were:
That warriors in Israel unbound their hair,
that the people came forward with a will,
for this, bless Yahweh!

and concludes:

So perish all your enemies, Yahweh!
And let those who love you be like the sun
when he arises in all his strength! [58]

The Lament of David for Saul and Jonathan

These songs and poems seem deliberately designed to give the people something they could easily remember. After all, it is easier to remember a folk song than a dusty passage of history.

David made this lament over Saul and his son Jonathan. It is written in the Book of the Just, so that it may be taught to the sons of Judah. It runs:

Alas, the glory of Israel has been slain on your
    heights!
How did the heroes fall?

---

[57] Numbers 21:27-30.

[58] Judges 5:1, 31.

Do not speak of it in Gath,
nor announce it in the streets of Ashkelon,
or the daughters of the Philistines will rejoice,
the daughters of the uncircumcised will gloat.

O mountains of Gilboa,
let there be no dew or rain on you;
treacherous fields,
for there the hero's shield was dishonored!

The shield of Saul was anointed not with oil
but with blood of the wounded, fat of the
     warriors;
the bow of Jonahean did not turn back,
nor the sword of Saul return idle.

Saul and Jonathan, loved and lovely,
neither in life, nor in death, were divided.
Swifter than eagles were they,
stronger were they than lions.

O daughters of Israel, weep for Saul
who clothed you in scarlet and fine linen,
who set brooches of gold
on your garments.

How did the heroes fall
in the thick of the battle?

O Jonathan, in your death I am stricken,
I am desolate for you, Jonathan my brother.
Very dear to me you were,
your love to me more wonderful
than the love of a woman.

How did the heroes fall
and the battle armor fail? [59]

---

[59] II Samuel 1:17-27.

The Psalms

It is almost impossible to treat this "worship book of the second temple" in a brief way! These songs were composed over a very long period of time, from before David through the Exile. They were collected into the form we have now for use in the temple when it was rebuilt after the Return. This book is extremely rich, demonstrating and preserving a whole range of human emotion. Here we find songs of joy (100, 103), confession (51), complaint (73), hate (58), confidence (23), and history (78).

Actually, the Book of Psalms is a collection of five distinct books, each concluding with a doxology, a statement of praise and thanksgiving. It is organized as follows:

Preface:	Psalms 1 and 2
Book I:	Psalms 3-41 with a concluding doxology 41:13
Book II:	Psalms 42-72, doxology 72:19
Book III:	Psalms 73-89, doxology 89:52
Book IV:	Psalms 90-106, doxology 106:48
Book V:	Psalms 107-149
Conclusion:	Psalm 150 (the whole Psalm is a doxology)

Another way to look at this poetic collection is to see that there are several different types of Psalms.

Personal Laments

Laments are one of the most common forms in the Psalms. They can be statements of trust, appeals to Yahweh for relief of a problem, or statements of obedience or thanksgiving. We can look at Psalm 13 as an example.

First, a sigh of one who has suffered:

> How much longer will you forget me, Yahweh?
>   Forever?
> How much longer will you hide your face from

me?
How much longer must I endure grief in my
    soul,
and sorrow in my heart by day and by night?
How much longer must my enemy have the
    upper hand of me?

Next, a petition:

Look and answer me, Yahweh my God!

Then, an intervention (cheer me up!):

Give my eyes light, or I shall sleep in death,
and my enemy will say, "I have beaten him,"
and my oppressors will have the joy of seeing me
    stumble.

Next, the "but" (a confession of faith):

But I for my part rely on your love, Yahweh;
let my heart rejoice in your saving help.

And finally, a promise (moving from lament to joy):

Let me sing to Yahweh for the goodness he
    has shown me. [60]

Personal Songs of Praise

One example is Psalm 9 and another is Psalm 66. I like this
one because it sounds so familiar. How many of us have made a
vow to God in the depth of some trouble, but how few follow
through when they are delivered. Here is a person who has had
some trouble. He enters the sanctuary bringing an offering, and he
proceeds to tell all around him, publicly, what Yahweh has done for
him:

---

[60] Psalm 13.

I bring holocausts to your house,
I bring them to fulfil those vows
that rose to my lips,
those vows I spoke when in trouble. . . .
Come and listen, all you who fear God,
while I tell you what he has done for me:
when I uttered my cry to him
and high praise was on my tongue,
had I been guilty in my heart,
the Lord would never have heard me.
But God not only heard me,
he listened to my prayer.
Blessed be God,
who neither ignored my prayer
nor deprived me of his love. [61]

National Laments and Songs of Praise

These are similar to personal laments, but the theme is the whole of Israel. A good example is Psalm 80. It includes a lament, verses 4-7; a contrast, verses 8-11; a "why," verses 12-17; and a vow of faithfulness, verses 18-19.

Psalm 24 is a fine example of a national song of praise.

General Hymns for Worship

One of my favorite hymns, and an especially beautifully written one is Psalm 8.

Yahweh, our Lord,
how great your name throughout the earth!

Above the heavens is your majesty chanted
by the mouths of children, babes in arms.
You set your stronghold firm against your foes

---

[61] Psalm 66:13, 16-20.

to subdue enemies and rebels.

I look up at your heavens, made by your
    fingers,
at the moon and stars you set in place
ah, what is man that you should spare a
    thought for him,
the son of man that you should care for him?

Yet you have made him little less than a god,
you have crowned him with glory and splendor,
made him lord over the work of your hands,
set all things under his feet,
sheep and oxen, all these,
yes, wild animals too,
birds in the air, fish in the sea
traveling the paths of the ocean.

Yahweh, our Lord,
how great your name throughout the earth!

Other poetic passages in the Psalms include:

Songs to be sung on a pilgrimage, especially on the walk
to the temple in Jerusalem, like Psalm 122;

Royal songs for crowning kings or for use before a war,
like Psalm 110; and

Wisdom songs, like Psalm 112.

The Song of Songs

This is a collection of romantic love songs. We should be
especially thankful that these neat folk songs and love ballads have
been preserved. They are frankly sexy; they survived only
because the early (and later) Christians interpreted them "allegorically" as referring to the love of God for his people and the love
of Jesus for the Church and the individual soul.

The themes range from "first love" through the dating period, the pain of separation (how many ways can you say goodby), to marriage.

Hallmark could learn from some of the verses:

Let him kiss me with the kisses of his mouth.
Your love is more delightful than wine;
delicate is the fragrance of your perfume,
your name is an oil poured out,
and that is why the maidens love you. [62]

I am the rose of Sharon,
the lily of the valleys.
As a lily among the thistles,
so is my love among the maidens.
As an apple tree among the trees of the orchard,
so is my Beloved among the young men.
In his longed-for shade I am seated
and his fruit is sweet to my taste.
He has taken me to his banquet hall,
and the banner he raises over me is love.
Feed me with apples,
for I am sick with love.
His left arm is under my head,
his right embraces me. [63]

Note how in this translation, *The Jerusalem Bible,* the word beloved in the third verse is capitalized. This betrays the uneasiness of some to truly let these be seen as love songs. It is an attempt to get readers to see them allegorically, that is to see the "beloved" as a spiritual figure. The New English Bible translation does not capitalize the word.

I hear my Beloved.
See how he comes
leaping on the mountains,

---

[62] Song of Songs 1:1-3.

[63] Song of Songs 2:1-6.

bounding over the hills.
My Beloved is like a gazelle,
like a young stag.
See where he stands
behind our wall.
He looks in at the window,
he peers through the lattice. [64]

How beautiful you are, my love,
how beautiful you are!
Your eyes, behind your veil,
are doves;
your hair is like a flock of goats
frisking down the slopes of Gilead.
Your teeth are like a flock of shorn ewes
as they come up from the wishing.
Each one has its twin,
not one unpaired with another.
Your lips are a scarlet thread
and your words enchanting.
Your cheeks, behind your veil,
are halves of pomegranate.
Your neck is the tower of David
built as a fortress,
hung round with a thousand bucklers,
and each the shield of a hero.
Your two breasts are two fawns,
twins of a gazelle,
that feed among the lilies.
Before the dawn-wind rises,
before the shadows flee,
I will go to the mountain of myrrh,
to the hill of frankincense.
You are wholly beautiful, my love,
and without a blemish. [65]

---

[64] Song of Songs 2:8-9.

[65] Song of Songs 4:1-7.

And if that is not enough, read 7:2-9!

Lamentations

This was written in Jerusalem, after the Fall in 586 B.C., and it was used as a liturgy afterward. It is really a collection of poems, individual and corporate laments. The first four are "alphabetical" verses, that is, each verse begins with a succeeding letter of the Hebrew alphabet.

All reflect the sorrow of the people over the "death" of Jerusalem, leading to confession of sin and the approval of Yahweh's judgment.

Chapter 3 is a personal lament, with the classical divisions: Despair, verses 1-20; hope, verses 21-39; response, verses 40-54; and prayer, verses 55-66.

> Yahweh, I called on your name
>   for the deep pit.
> You heard me crying, "do not close
>   your ear to my prayer."
> You came near that day when I called
>   to you;
> you said, "Do not be afraid."

Reading this lament strikes a lot of responsive chords in a sensitive person. Too bad it is "lost" or so long neglected.

Chapter 4

Philosophy

These books are often referred to as "wisdom books," and some definitions from Webster may be helpful:

> WISDOM: The ability to judge soundly and deal sagaciously with facts, especially as they relate to life and conduct; knowledge with the capacity to make due use of it; perception of the best ends and the best means; discernment and judgment.

> WISDOM LITERATURE: The wisdom of these writings [in the Old Testament] consists in detached sage utterances on concrete issues of life, without effort at philosophical systems.

In our current understanding of philosophical divisions, these books might be described as pragmatic philosophy, but I prefer to call them wisdom.

Proverbs

Webster defines a proverb as "a profound maxim, a sage sentence, a truth couched obscurely." But I call the Book of Proverbs a collection of the words of Jewish mothers to long-suffering children! It is the collected wisdom and teaching of home, temple, court, and school.

There are three major divisions in the book: Poems, chapters 1-9; epigrams, chapters 10-29; and an appendix, chapters 30-31. What follows are some of my favorite proverbs, arranged by the themes they express.

On the Calvinist work ethic:

Idler, go to the ant;
    ponder her ways and grow wise:
no one gives her orders,
    no overseer, no master,
yet all through the summer she makes sure of her food,
    and gathers her supplies at harvest time.
How long do you intend to lie there, idler?
    When are you going to rise from your sleep?
A little sleep, a little drowsiness,
    a little folding of the arms to take life easier,
and like a vagrant, poverty is at your elbow
    and, like a beggar, want. [66]

On fatherly advice (how does he know so much?):

My son, keep my words
    and treasure my principles, . . .

Call perception your dearest friend,
    to preserve you from the alien woman,
from the stranger, with her wheedling words.
From the window of her house
    she looked out on the street,
to see if among the men, young and callow,
    there was one young man who had no sense
    at all.
And now he passes down the lane, and comes
    near her corner,
    reaching the path to her house
at twilight when day is declining,
    at dead of night and in the dark.
But look, the woman comes to meet him,
    dressed like a harlot, wrapped in a veil.
She is loud and brazen;
    her feet cannot rest at home.
Now in the street, now in the square,
    she is on the look-out at every corner.

---

[66] Proverbs 6:6-11.

She catches hold of him, she kisses him,
    the bold-faced creature says to him,
"I had to offer sacrifices:
    I discharged my vows today,
that is why I came out to meet you,
    to look for you, and now I have found you.
I have made my bed gay with quilts,
    spread the best Egyptian sheets,
I have sprinkled my bed with myrrh,
    with aloes and with cinnamon.
Come, let us drink deep of love until the
    morning,
    and abandon ourselves to delight.
For my husband is not at home,
    he has gone on a very long journey,
taking his moneybags with him;
    he will not be back until the moon is full."
With her persistent coaxing she entices him,
    draws him on with her seductive patter.
Bemused, he follows her
    like an ox being led to the slaughter. . . . [67]

On church bureaucrats (in Today's English Version):

It is better to meet a mother bear
    robbed of her cubs
than to meet some fool
    busy with a stupid project. [68]

On fathers and mothers for their children:

The eye which looks jeeringly on a father,
    and scornfully on an ageing mother,

---

[67] Proverbs 7:1, 4-27.

[68] Proverbs 17:12.

shall be pecked out by the ravens of the valley,
   and eaten by the vultures. [69]

Of course, there is also that magnificent poem on the "perfect" wife, an alphabetical poem, Proverbs 31:10-31. However, in deference to my feminist commitment I will not include it in this text.

Job

The Book of Job is a classically beautiful piece of wisdom literature in poetic form. There is no identification of the writer and much dispute about the time of its composition. The core of the story may be older than the written form.

In the Book of Job, the author deals with one of the hardest questions we can ask: Why does a just and loving God permit the innocent to suffer? But we sometimes fail to see that Job tackles another issue. He opens a discussion that we desperately need in our time, when he makes the point that prosperity and adversity have no connection with goodness and wickedness.

In a dramatic way Job is the example, par excellance, of the good man, but he looses all his material possessions! His writing was a reaction against other "wisdom literature," particularly against the proverbs where the motivation to live a good life is the promise of material blessing.

An outline of Job's speeches may be helpful:

Introduction: 1:1-2:13 (in prose form)
Job's lament: 3

	Eliphaz	Job	Bildad	Job	Zophar	Job
1st cycle	4-5	6-7	8	9-10	11	12-14
2nd cycle	15	16-17	18	19	20	21
3rd cycle	22	23	only fragments of the rest			

Yahweh and Job: 38-41

---

[69] Proverbs 30:17.

Job's Answer: 40:3-5; 42:2-6
Closing: 42:7-17 (again in prose form)

Some marvelous literary expressions occur throughout the book, but my favorite is in Yahweh's speech to Job:

Who is this obscuring my designs
    with his empty-headed words?
Brace yourself like a fighter;
    now it is my turn to ask questions and yours
    to inform me.
Where were you when I laid the earth's foundations?
    Tell me, since you are so well-informed!
Who decided the dimensions of it, do you know?
    Or who stretched the measuring line across
    it?
What supports its pillars at their bases?
    Who laid its cornerstone
when all the stars of the morning were singing
    with joy. . . .

Have you ever in your life given orders to the
    morning
    or sent the dawn to its post,
telling it to grasp the earth by its edges
    and shake the wicked out of it, . . .

Have you ever visited the place where the snow is kept,
    or seen where the hail is stored up, . . .

Can you fasten the harness of the Pleiades,
    or untie Orion's bands. . . .

Does the hawk take flight on your advice
    when he spreads his wings to travel south?
Does the eagle soar at your command
    to make her eyrie in the heights? [70]

---

[70] Job 38:2-6, 12-13, 22, 31, 39:26-28.

On and on it goes like this until Job replies:

> My words have been frivolous: what can I
>   reply?
> I had better lay my finger on my lips.
>
> I have spoken once. . . . I will not speak again;
>   more than once. . . . I will add nothing. [71]

And later:

> I know that you are all-powerful:
>   what you conceive, you can perform.
> I am the man who obscured your designs
>   with my empty-headed words.
> I have been holding forth on matters I cannot
>   understand,
>   on marvels beyond me and my knowledge.
> I knew you then only by hearsay;
>   but now, having seen you with my own eyes,
> I retract all I have said,
>   and in dust and ashes I repent. [72]

Ecclesiastes

This book was written about 200 B.C. The author is unknown to us. He is called "Qoheleth, son of David, King in Jerusalem," but the word *qoheleth* itself means "one who speaks in an assembly." It is for that reason that some in the past have called him "preacher," but I wonder why not "high school principal"! After all, such a one speaks in an assembly!

---

[71] Job 40:4-5.

[72] Job 42:2-6.

This writer says the material is Solomon's, but that is a code word or symbol for all wisdom writings. We feel this writer was a Jew and one influenced by the Greek culture. Remember that by now the country was ruled by Greeks (Alexander had conquered it by 332 B.C.). The Book of Ecclesiastes is divided into two parts: Chapters 1-6 are poems; and chapters 7-12 are proverbs and epigrams. In both sections the key word is vanity. Like Job, the writer breaks with the tradition that being materially prosperous is a sign of Yahweh's blessing and vice versa. The rich are NOT always happy.

Most of us knew Ecclesiastes 3:1-8 even before Bob Dylan made money by setting it to music:

There is a season for everything, a time for
    every occupation under heaven:
A time for giving birth,
a time for dying;
a time for planting,
a time for uprooting what has been planted.
A time for killing,
a time for healing;
a time for knocking down,
a time for building.
A time for tears,
a time for laughter;
a time for mourning
a time for dancing.
A time for throwing stones away,
a time for gathering them up;
a time for embracing,
a time to refrain from embracing.
A time for searching,
a time for losing;
a time for keeping,
a time for throwing away.
A time for tearing,
a time for sewing;
a time for keeping silent,
a time for speaking.
A time for loving,

a time for hating;
a time for war,
a time for peace. [73]

This rather pessimistic, fatalistic poem breaks with the usual world view of the Jews. Instead of seeing the hand of God in history it tends to support the view of endless cycles in history. Perhaps this is why the book had some trouble being accepted as part of the cannon and was not admitted until well after the time of Jesus.

The phrase translated here as "There is a season for everything," carries the meaning in Hebrew that "Everything is under inexorable law." Some have used this scripture to justify the idea that anything may be right under certain circumstances and read it as a blank check in ethical matters, but that interpretation cannot be sustained by any accurate translation.

Chapters 11 and 12 are sober reflections on life, including such statements as:

Cast your bread on the water; at long last you will find it again. Share with seven, yes with eight, for you never know what disaster may occur on earth.

Rejoice in your youth, you who are young;
let your heart give you joy in your young days.
Follow the promptings of your heart
and the desires of your eyes.

Yet youth, the age of dark hair, is vanity. And remember your creator in the days of your youth, before evil days come and the years approach when you say, "These give me no pleasure," before sun and light and moon and stars grow dark, and the clouds return after the rain;

before the silver cord has snapped,
or the golden lamp been broken,

---

[73] Ecclesiastes 3:1-8.

or the pitcher shattered at the spring,
or the pulley cracked at the well,
or before the dust returns to the earth
    as it once came from it,
and the breath to God who gave it. [74]

Here too is a good thought, a sober thought, about money:

He who loves money never has money enough,
he who loves wealth never has enough profit;
    this, too is vanity. [75]

---

[74] Ecclesiastes 11:1-2, 9, 12:1-2, 6-7.

[75] Ecclesiastes 5:9.

Chapter 5

Short Stories

Some fine examples of fiction and short-story writing are found in the Old Testament. They have been studied as serious literature for centuries. In them we find a truth imparted through the telling of an imaginative story.

Some of the best of this material is found in the part of the Old Testament called the Megilloth. The word Megilloth, which means "scrolls" in Hebrew, is used to identify five quite diverse Old Testament books which were used as special readings at certain annual festivals. They are:

Ruth	read at	the Feast of Weeks
Song of Songs	read at	Passover
Ecclesiastes	read at	the Feast of Tabernacles
Lamentations	read at	the Commemoration of the Fall of Jerusalem
Esther	read at	Purim

Ruth

This book is set in the period of the Judges (1150-1000 B.C.) but was probably not written in its present form until after the Exile, perhaps as late as 250 B.C.

Its purpose is to explain how a Moabite woman (a non-Jew) came to be an ancestress of King David. Another purpose may have been to counteract the strict ruling of Nehemiah who forbade the returning Jews to intermarry with any others, especially the Samaritans. Some of the returning Jews had created new and serious problems by marrying women not of Jewish descent. Ezra had ordered such men to divorce these wives and put away the children they had by them. He and Nehemiah felt that the people had lived so long in "unclean" lands that they had become lax in their religious practices. This harsh action caused great unhappiness and injustice. But this theme of racial exclusiveness is delivered a hard blow by recalling that a complete outsider was the great grand-mother of David.

Most people recognize the words of Ruth to Naomi, her mother-in-law, when Naomi tells Ruth to go back to her own people while she will return the land of her husband:

> Naomi said to her, "Look, your sister-in-law has gone back to her people and her god. You must return too."
> But Ruth said, "Do not press me to leave you and to turn back from your company, for wherever you go, I will go, wherever you live, I will live. Your people shall be my people, and your God, my God. [76]

Jonah

This small book traditionally has been gathered with the "Twelve Minor Prophets." While it is reputed to be the story of a prophet, it contains no prophetic deliverances such as the ones we looked at earlier.

As in the Book of Ruth, the major theme is that of speaking against the rising exclusivism of the late post-Exile age. It is a tremendous parable, equal to any told by Jesus, attacking head-on the narrow nationalism of the Judaism of the day.

The outline is familiar: First, Jonah gets an unpopular assign-ment and decides not to carry it out; then he surrenders to the judgment of God via the storm and is thrown into the sea, where he finds himself in a tight spot; next, he is rescued, gives thanks, gets his commission again, and goes to carry it out; finally, he again rebels after delivering his message and observing the mercy of God and is again rebuked.

Certain passages deserve to be quoted here. Jonah's reaction to his "tight place" is one that many can find familiar:

---

[76] Ruth 1:15-16.

Out of my distress I cried to Yahweh
and he answered me;
from the belly of Sheol I cried,
and you have heard my voice.
You cast me into the abyss, into the heart of
    the sea,
and the flood surrounded me.
All your waves, your billows,
washed over me.

The waters surrounded me right to my throat,
the abyss was all around me.
The seaweed was wrapped round my head
at the roots of the mountains.
I went down into the countries underneath the
    earth,
to the peoples of the past.
But you lifted my life from the pit,
    Yahweh, my God. [77]

The climax, the real lesson, is told in just a few magnificent phrases from the mouth of Yahweh:

You are only upset about a castor-oil plant which cost you no labor, which you did not make grow, which sprouted in a night and has perished in a night. And am I not to feel sorry for Nineveh, the great city, in which there are more than a hundred and twenty thousand people who cannot tell their right hand from their left, to say nothing of all the animals? [78]

Those of our day, who persist in putting property and profit before people could learn from that little couplet!

---

[77] Jonah 2:3-7.

[78] Jonah 4:10-11.

Esther

The Book of Esther is almost the flip side of Jonah. It not only extols nationalism, it provides a pattern that has been loved and cherished by many. Even though the book never mentions Yahweh and is devoid of religious matters, it has been highly regarded by the Jewish community from the time of the Maccabees to the present day.

The story is set in the time of Persian rule, but may have been written much later, perhaps during the time of oppression under Greek rule. Some would call this the Book of Mordecai, for he is the brains behind the scheme to save the Jews from a "final solution," the elimination of those people who refused to be assimilated into Persian culture.

Esther, a Jewess, becomes queen and is used by Mordecai to win the reprieve of the whole people from extinction. In celebration of this deliverance the feast of Purim was established. Thus this book is really a festival legend. Its inclusion in the Old Testament has been hotly debated by both Jews and Christians. Luther, for instance, rejected it vehemently for its theme of vengeance not by Yahweh but by humans.

The flavor of the story is seen in this vignette. Mordecai has instructed Esther to do his bidding and she is wavering. She says:

> All the king's servants and the people of his provinces know that for a man or woman who approaches the inner court without being summoned there is one penalty: death, unless, by pointing his golden scepter towards him, the king grants him his life. And I have not been summoned to the king for the last thirty days.

These words of Esther were reported to Mordecai, who sent back the following reply:

> Do not suppose that, because you are in the king's palace, you are going to escape. No. If you persist in remaining silent at such a time, relief and deliverance will come to the Jews from another place, but both you and the house

of your father will perish. Who knows? Perhaps you
have come to the throne for just such a time as this. [79]

Daniel

This was the last book of the Old Testament to be written. It
was composed during the Maccabean war. This book could be
classified as apocalyptic literature for it bears a striking resemb-
lance to the Book of Revelation. Both were written during a time
of persecution and both used "code" words and concepts to get
across their message of courage.

The Book of Daniel is set in the time of the Babylonian exile,
but it really provides the rationale for the Maccabean revolution in
168-165 B.C. I sometimes characterize Daniel as the "Indiana Jones
of the Old Testament" because he has so many adventures! For
parents who want their children to eat healthful food, here is the
story. Daniel and his friends were to be trained for service to King
Nebuchadnezzar. They were expected to eat the food from the
king's table (a real opportunity to eat high off the hog), but they
refuse. Here is the dialogue:

> "Please allow your servants a ten days' trial, during
> which we are given only vegetables to eat and water to
> drink. You can then compare our looks with those of the
> boys who eat the king's food; go by what you see, and
> treat your servants accordingly." The man agreed to do
> what they asked and put them on ten days' trial. When
> the ten days were over they looked and were in better
> health than any of the boys who had eaten their al-
> lowance from the royal table; so the guard withdrew their
> allowance of food and the wine they were to drink, and
> gave them vegetables. And God favored these four boys

---

[79] Esther 4:10-14.

with knowledge and intelligence in everything connected with literature and in wisdom. [80]

So eat your vegetables!

---

[80] Daniel 1:12-17.

Part II

The New Testament

Chapter 6

Introduction to the New Testament

As we move now to the New Testament books, we must keep in mind the principles we laid down for our study:

How you interpret a piece of the Bible depends on the type of writing it is.

All translations are interpretations.

There is a correlation between the way people think, act, write, and live and the land upon which they live.

People tend to pattern their religious understanding in relation to their type of social organization.

In addition it is essential to remember that the early Christian church came directly out of the Jewish religious community. For the most part the followers of Jesus were regular synagogue attenders and met in the synagogue until they were forced to go elsewhere. When they did go elsewhere to meet, they took with them their sacred writings, the Old Testament, the books we have just discussed.

I feel certain that those who began to write about the way of life set forth by Jesus had no thought that their writings would one day become part of the sacred literature that provided their base of understanding of Yahweh. Paul certainly had no thought of this, as we shall see from his letters.

The writing of the New Testament writings came well after the fact of Jesu's life and teachings. It was the demand of the growing church, and especially of the non-Jews, for information about Jewish tradition, customs, and history and about the life of the one called Jesus that inspired what we now have. Further we must remember that the Bible of Jesus was the Old Testament. He studied it and knew it well, as did many of his followers.

All this gives us some insight into why the authors of the New Testament were so concerned to align the new perceptions of Jesus with the Jewish sacred writings. They had experienced a time of transformation with Jesus and in a most natural way, were reluctant to let go of the past.

It is also important to realize that the New Testament covers a much shorter period of history (only about 100 years) than the more than 1,700 years included in the Old Testament.

Historical Interlude

The historical setting for the events described in the New Testament can be breifly summarized as follows:

> After the brief independence of the Maccabean period (165-63 B.C.), the ROMANS, under POMPEY, asserted tight control of Jerusalem in 63 B.C.
>
> The HEROD family gained control of the puppet government.
>
> HEROD saw to it that the Temple was repaired.
>
> PONTIUS PILATE became procurator of Judea in 26 A.D.
>
> JESUS was executed in 30 A. D.
>
> PENTECOST, the "birth of the church," occurred a few weeks later.
>
> PAUL was converted from being a Pharisee to the way of life of Jesus in 36 or 37 A.D.; he died in 67 A.D.

JEWISH REVOLTS AGAINST THE ROMANS
started in 66 A.D.

TITUS laid seige to Jerusalem in 70 A.D. and
destroyed the Temple.

MASADA held out until 73 A.D.

A SECOND JEWISH REBELLION occurred
under Bar Cocheba in 132-135 A.D.

JERUSALEM was recaptured in 134 A.D. and
the Temple was made into a shrine to Zeus.

Geographic Interlude

With the New Testament, the geographic scene shifts from the
Fertile Crescent to the Mediterranean Sea. Favored beyond all
other great bodies of water by climate and position, this mil-
lion-square-mile sea of coves and arms and islets has a human
measure. Plato said, "like frogs around a pond we have settled
down upon the shores of this sea."

This sea in the midst of lands unites and divides three
continents. The mighty Xerxes once had it lashed three hundred
strokes because a storm on the Hellespont wrecked his invasion
fleet. By its shores Greeks and Phoenicians founded a hundred
thirty famed cities, from Massilia (present Marseille) and Malaca
(present Malaga) to Naples and Syracuse. The city-state of Carthage in North Africa was already collecting the equivolent of $43
million in tariffs and annual tributes in the third century B.C.

The Latin root of the word Mediterranean means "the middle of
the world." The Romans called it "our sea," as their ships sailed
regularly from Alexandria to Gibraltar with all sorts of cargo.

Chapter 7

The Letters of Paul

Letters are the earliest type of writing we have in the New Testament. Letters then were pretty much like letters now. Most were a continuation in writing of a conversation or teaching that had occurred earlier. Some were written specifically to answer questions raised by the gatherings of new Christians.

Paul wrote a total of ten letters from three different places:

	Letter#	To	Date A.D.
From Corinth	1	Thessalonians	50
	2	Thessalonians	51
	6	Galatians	56
	7	Romans	57
From Ephesus	3	Corinthians	56
	4	Corinthians	57
	5	Philippians	57
From Rome	8	Colossians	62
	9	Philemon	62
	10	Ephesians	62

Paul wrote these letters in common everyday Greek, and for the most part they were very informal. We know that Paul was a Jew who could speak Hebrew even though he lived in Tarsus (in present day Turkey), and that he knew the sacred writings intimately. He was a trained rabbi from the upper class and was conservative in outlook. He was a Roman citizen and proud of it, though he was well educated in the Greek tradition.

It helps me right off to know that Paul was not infallible. His letters were an early attempt at communicating the message of Jesus' way of life, and he obviously botched it. But his errors were natural, and of the sort that any might have made. Paul was learning as he went along. He did not leap full-blown onto center stage.

Paul went through years of trying one thing after another, gradually maturing in his understanding of Jesus and his teaching. Watch, then, how he matures in these letters written over fifteen years of his life. Try to grasp his internal struggle with new concepts as he interprets them in new situations.

I and II Thessalonians

Paul preached three Sabbaths in the synagogue at Thessalonica (in present-day Greece) where he

argued with them, quoting texts of Scripture which he expounded and applied to show that the Messiah had to suffer and rise form the dead. "And this Jesus," he said, "whom I am proclaiming to you, is the Messiah." [1]

Not all the Jews, by any means, were convinced, and after he left, there was a great deal of dispute in the community. But Paul obviously had talked about Jesus' return, and he had done it so persuasively that some of the people had stopped working and were just waiting around for the event to happen! Paul then wrote two letters, possibly within a month of each other, to put Jesus' return in better perspective and to encourage people to live more normal and productive lives while they waited.

These are our orders to you, brothers, in the name of our Lord Jesus Christ: hold aloof from every Christian brother who falls into idle habits, and does not follow the tradition you received from us. You know yourselves how you ought to copy our example: we were no idlers among you; we did not accept board and lodging from anyone without paying for it; we toiled and drudged, we worked for a living night and day, rather than be a burden to

---

[1] Acts 17:2-3 (By reading the book of Acts we know where Paul went and with whom).

any of you--not because we have not the right to maintenance, but to set an example for you to imitate.

For even during our stay with you we laid down the rule: the man who will not work shall not eat. We mention this because we hear that some of your number are idling their time away, minding everybody's business but their own. To all such we give these orders, and we appeal to them in the name of the Lord Jesus Christ to work quietly for their living. [2]

I and II Corinthians

Many scholars believe that Paul may have written a total of four letters to the group of Christians called Corinthians: One on sexual immorality (lost except for a fragment in II Corinthians 6:13-7:1); the letter in I Corinthians; a "sharp" letter, probably II Corinthians 10-13; and the letter found in II Corinthians 1-9.

The letter of I Corinthians was obviously a response to a number of questions. Paul writes here in a rather logical order to answer them:

Problem	Text	Solution
Unity	1:10-4:21	Pull together, 4:12.
Immorality	5:	Drive out the wicked among you, 5:13.
Law suits in civil courts	6:1-11	Don't, 6:7.
Immorality	6:12-20	Glorify God in your body, 6:20.
Marriage	7:	Be sensitive, 7:1-5.
Freedom	8-11:1	All is lawful but not all is helpful, 10:23.
Women in church	11:2-16	Wear veils, 11:10.

---

[2] II Thessalonians 6-12.

Decorum at the	11:16-34	Dignity, 11:23.
Lord's Supper		
Individualism	12-14	Make love your aim, 14:1.
Resurrection	15	All are made alive, 15:22.

Paul had great gifts as a pastor to take such time and effort with these people. But, some people were going about criticizing him, saying he was a heretic, tearing down his character, trying to discredit his credentials. What did it cost? Listen:

> But if there is to be bravado (and here I speak as a fool), I can indulge in it too. Are they Hebrews? So am I. Israelites? So am I. Abraham's descendants? So am I. Are they servants of Christ? I am made to speak like this, but I can outdo them. More over-worked than they, scourged more severely, more often imprisoned, many a time face to face with death. Five times the Jews have given me the thirty-nine strokes; three times I have been beaten with rods; once I was stoned; three times I have been shipwrecked, and for twenty-four hours I was adrift on the open sea. I have been constantly on the road; I have met dangers from rivers, dangers from robbers, dangers from my fellow countrymen, dangers from foreigners, dangers in towns, dangers in the country, dangers at sea, dangers from false friends. I have toiled and drudged; I have often gone without sleep; hungry and thirsty, I have often gone fasting; and I have suffered from cold and exposure.
> Apart from these external things, there is the responsibility that weighs on me every day, my anxious concern for all our congregations. If anyone is weak, do I not share his weakness? If anyone is made to stumble, does my heart not blaze with indignation? [3]

That list ought to stop anyone from complaining!

_____

[3] II Corinthians 11:21-29.

Philippians

There is a real dispute as to the date of this letter and the place from which it is written. The traditional view held that it was written late, that it was perhaps Paul's last letter, and that Paul was in prison in Rome at the time he wrote it. Newer scholarship places it as one of the letters written from a jail in Ephesus in 57 A.D. I accept the latter view, mostly because it makes more sense. For instance, Paul speaks of frequent visits or at least "contacts" with the people of Philippi while he is in prison. This makes sense when we consider that the two towns are reasonably close to each other, and it seems more reasonable than thinking of the Philippians taking a long sea journey to Rome to visit Paul. At any rate, the important thing to know is that the letter was written while Paul was in prison. This is important because the letter is full of joy and thanksgiving, things that one does not normally associate with being chained in prison!

Paul makes several points in this letter:

Thank you, Philippians, for being you and for the gift (whatever it was).

I am sending Epaphroditus back home. Thanks for sending him to keep me company. He has done a great job of that, but his health worries me and I think he ought to be at home.

I want to encourage you to have faith as you go through your trials and persecutions there in Philippi.

For God's sake strive for unity among yourselves. There are enough enemies trying to split you from the outside!

Most scholars feel that Paul has preserved for us one of the early hymns of the church in this letter:

For the divine nature was his from the first; yet he did not think to snatch at equality with God, but made

himself nothing, assuming the nature of a slave. Bearing
the human likeness, revealed in human shape, he humbled
himself, and in obedience accepted even death--death on a
cross. Therefore, God raised him to the heights and
bestowed on him the name above all names, that at the
name of Jesus every knee should bow--in heaven, on
earth, and in the depths--and every tongue confess, "Jesus
Christ is Lord," to the glory of God the Father. [4]

Galatians

Paul was always having to defend himself and the new church
from the Jews who did not accept his claim that Jesus was indeed
the awaited Messiah. Sometimes they attack him personally calling
into question his credentials. In this letter we see clearly this
conflict. Paul becomes quite sharp when people seem to listen to
his detractors:

You stupid Galatians! You must have been bewitched--you
before whose eyes Jesus Christ was openly displayed upon
his cross! Answer me one question: did you receive the
Spirit by keeping the law or by believing the gospel
message? Can it be that you are so stupid? [5]

The real question was whether this new Christian movement
coming right out of the Jewish tradition should be seen as a sect of
Judaism or as a separate movement. Should new converts, for
instance, submit to the initiation rite of circumcision? Must you
first be a Jew in order to become a Christian?
So here Paul, the former Pharisee, discusses Jewish law and the
freedom of the followers of Jesus. Perhaps this was the turning
point. From this time on the followers of Jesus must leave the
synagogues and establish their own places of meeting.

---

[4] Philippians 2:6-11 .

[5] Galatians 3:1-3.

At any rate, Paul by this time was convinced that what Jesus had done was to make a radical departure from the past. This was not to be seen as a mere reform within Judaism but as truly something new. In ringing words he says:

> Christ set us free, to be free men. Stand firm, then, and refuse to be tied to the yoke of slavery again. [6]

But he goes on to caution:

> . . . only do not turn your freedom into licence. [7]

And then he concludes:

> Circumcision is nothing; uncircumcision is nothing; the only thing that counts is new creation! [8]

No wonder the conservatives were out to get him!

Romans

I am convinced that this letter to the Romans must be seen in the light of the letter to the Galatians, in which Paul reacted quickly to the problems of law and freedom and shot from the hip. He must have thought about that a great deal after he sent the letter, for just a short time later, we find him composing a more balanced letter on the same subject. He sends it to the church in Rome as a prelude to his coming there for the first time. Since he does not know anyone in Rome personally it is less "personal" than the other letters.

Paul's point is that neither the wisdom of the Greeks nor the law of the Jews can save a person, only the free gift of God, which

---

[6] Galatians 5:1 .

[7] Galatians 5:13.

[8] Galatians 6:15.

he calls grace. You are set right with God, or justified to use the technical term, by your faith in the fact that God already loves you, forgives you, accepts you. Again, you must remember that Paul wrote within the framework of his world and experience.

I think Paul is at his best when he lets go of his academic logic and soars in such passages as the following:

> With all this in mind, what are we to say? If God is on our side, who is against us? He did not spare his own Son, but gave him up for us all; and with this gift how can he fail to lavish upon us all he has to give? Who will be the accuser of God's chosen ones? It is God who pronounces acquittal; then who can condemn? It is Christ--Christ who died, and, more than that, was raised from the dead--who is at God's right hand, and indeed pleads our cause. Then what can separate us from the love of Christ? Can affliction or hardship? Can persecution, hunger, nakedness, peril, or the sword? . . . in spite of all, overwhelming victory is ours through him who loved us. For I am convinced that there is nothing in death or life, in the realm of spirits or superhuman powers, in the world as it is or the world as it shall be, in the forces of the universe, in heights or depths--nothing in all creation that can separate us from the love of God in Christ Jesus our Lord. [9]

Even though many books have been written about Paul's missionary journeys, we do not know for certain how and when they were made. However, some things about him are clear.

After his conversion he was a zealot in trying to spread the good news about Jesus, and he was not afraid to take on the Jews in the synagogue nor, for that matter, the public officials in some of the towns. There was a determined effort on the part of at least some of the traditionalists to stop Paul at any cost. Some time after writing to the Romans he left Corinth for Jerusalem, where he was arrested on the charge of disturbing the peace. He allegedly had allowed non-believers to come into the temple with him. He was jailed for perhaps as much as three years. He used his

---

[9] Romans 8:31-39.

Roman citizenship to appeal his case and was permitted to go to Rome to make his case before the emperor. He was taken to Rome and again placed in prison.

Colossians

This letter, and the one to the Ephesians which is very much like it, were definitely written from the prison in Rome and are referred to as the "captivity letters." The letters were sent to congregations that Paul had founded about ten years before in present-day Turkey.

The main problem dealt with was the rise of a heresy called gnosticism, a mixture of many different religious trends in which Jesus was seen as simply one of many "powers" between God and the human. All you needed, said these teachers, was the proper knowledge and you would understand the secret of salvation.

To Paul the "secret" was constantly and clearly made known by the prophets and supremely through Jesus. The key passage is:

The task assigned to me by God for your benefit [is] to deliver his message in full; to announce the secret hidden

for long ages and through many generations, but now
disclosed to God's people, to whom it was his will to
make it known--to make known how rich and glorious it
is among all nations. The secret is this: Christ in you,
the hope of a glory to come. [10]

Paul clearly understood that the church was the continuing
vehicle that would make this known to all. He proposed, therefore,
a very high view of the church. He saw it as the way persons
become knowledgeable in the gospel.

Therefore, since Jesus was delivered to you as Christ and
Lord, live your lives in union with him. Be rooted in
him; be built in him; be consolidated in the faith you
were taught; let your hearts overflow with thankfulness.
Be on your guard; do not let your minds be captured by
hollow and delusive speculations, based on traditions of
man-made teaching and centered on the elemental spirits
of the universe and not on Christ. [11]

Ephesians

This letter is similar to the letter to the Colossians. Haven't
you written almost the same letter to two persons? But while
Colossians is choppy in its style, Ephesians is more flowing.
Paul is encouraging them with his declaration of the high
purpose of the followers of Jesus:

So he came and proclaimed the good news: peace to you
who were far off, and peace to those who were near by;
for through him we both alike have access to the Father
in the one Spirit. Thus you are no longer aliens in a
foreign land, but fellow-citizens with God's people,
members of God's household. You are built upon the

---

[10] Colossians 1:25-27.

[11] Colossians 2:6-8.

foundations laid by the apostles and prophets, and Christ
Jesus himself is the foundation-stone. In him the whole
building is bonded together and grows into a holy temple
in the Lord. In him you too are being built with all the
rest into a spiritual dwelling for God. [12]

And he entreats them to live at peace with one another, using their
gifts for the building up of the church:

> As God has called you, live up to your calling. Be humble
> always and gentle, and patient too. Be forgiving with one
> another and charitable. Spare no effort to make fast with
> the bonds of peace the unity which the Spirit gives.
> There is one body and one Spirit, as there is also one
> hope held out in God's call to you; one Lord, one faith,
> one baptism; one God and Father of all, who is over all
> and through all and in all. [13]

But Paul becomes quite assertive in this letter and uses
military images to show how they are to take courage and stand
against their foes:

> Finally, then, find your strength in the Lord, in his
> mighty power. Put on all the armor which God provides,
> so that you may be able to stand firm against the devices
> of the devil. For our fight is not against human foes, but
> against cosmic powers, against the authorities and
> potentates of this dark world, against the superhuman
> forces of evil in the heavens. Therefore, take up God's
> armor; then you will be able to stand your ground when
> things are at their worst, to complete every task and still
> to stand. Stand firm, I say. Fasten on the belt of truth;
> for a coat of mail put on integrity; let the shoes on your
> feet be the gospel of peace, to give you firm footing; and
> with all these, take up the great shield of faith, with
> which you will be able to quench all the flaming arrows

---

[12] Ephesians 2:17-22.

[13] Ephesians 4:1-6.

of the evil one. Take salvation for helmet; for sword, take that which the Spirit gives you--the words that come from God. Give yourselves wholly to prayer and entreaty; pray on every occasion in the power of the Spirit. To this end keep watch and persevere, always interceding for all God's people . . . .[14]

Philemon

If the preceding are letters, Philemon is a postcard, and it's pure Paul. The subject of this missive is the return of a runaway slave, Onesimus, to his master, Philemon. Paul unfortunately does not speak against slavery in this correspondence, but does say that both slave and master are Christians and therefore have a different relationship than before! One can only conjecture how often it happened that in the new congregations a "master" found himself taking communion from the hands of one of his "slaves" and then all being called together to be "slaves for Jesus Christ."

So this new Christian, Paul, worked and taught in the midst of a changing world, with a maturing theology and a growing view of the church. He confronted severe problems of understanding among the new converts, he battled the traditionalists, he fended off the government, all while he himself was maturing in the faith! Remember, he was not an academic Christian. He knew well the Old Testament roots and scripture, but he was new in the way of life modeled by Jesus, and no one had formed a church before him, so he had no model to see.

Somehow he almost always turned the problems he dealt with into statements that give glory to God in a most unusual way. For example, the Corinthians were acting like pigs at the Lord's table and from this come the words:

---

[14] Ephesians 6:10-18

For the tradition which I handed on to you came to me from the Lord himself: that the Lord Jesus, on the night of his arrest, took bread and, after giving thanks to God, broke it and said: "This is my body, which is for you; do this as a memorial of me." [15]

On another occasion, an ugly dispute arose among some as to what kind of activity was more important. That led to:

About the gifts of the Spirit, there are some things of which I do not wish you to remain ignorant . . . you are Christ's body, and each of you a limb or organ of it . . . and now I will show you the best way of all. . . . If I speak in tongues of men and angels but have not love, I am a sounding gong or a clanging cymbal. I may have the gift of prophecy, and know every hidden truth; I may have faith strong enough to move mountains; but if I have no love, I am nothing. I may dole out all I possess, or even give my body to be burnt, but if I have no love, I am none the better.

Love is patient; love is knind and envies no one. Love is never boastful, nor conceited, nor rude; never selfish, not quick to take offence. Love keeps no score of wrongs; does not gloat over other men's sins, but delights in the truth. There is nothing love cannot face; there is no limit to its faith, its hope and its endurance. . . . In a word, there are three thnings that last for ever: faith, hope, and love; but the greatest of them all is love. Put love first. . . . [16]

---

[15] I Corinthians 11:22-24.

[16] I Corinthians 12:1-14:1 (selections).

Chapter 8

The Gospels

It is clear that the earliest Christians felt little need for a written account of the life of Jesus. They, for the most part, had lived with him or been with him at significant times. Many others had heard about him and had his words quoted verbatim to them by his intimate companions. As in Old Testament times, this was still a time of largely illiterate people, and the gift of telling a story or quoting a person's words was still undisturbed by copying of documents. It was essential to remember what you saw, heard, or were told and to be able to pass it on accurately. Still another reason why a written record did not seem important to these people was the widespread belief that Jesus would return again during their own lifetime.

But as the Church spread further throughout the Mediterranean world, it attracted more and more people who had not had a Jewish background, and some written "norms" were deemed necessary. Obviously a number of persons did some writing to describe the life and record the words of Jesus. Luke opens his gospel with the statement:

> Many writers have undertaken to draw up an account of the events that have happened among us, following the traditions handed down to us by the original eyewitnesses and servants of the Gospel. And so I in my turn . . . as one who has gone over the whole course of these events in detail, have decided to write a connected narrative for you, so as to give you authentic knowledge about the matters of which you have been informed. [17]

We know that early on there were small pieces of the activity and the words of Jesus written down by a variety of people. These,

---

[17] Luke 1:1-4.

along with the oral accounts, were passed around. But Mark apparently was the first to gather some of these and to compose the first account of the life of Jesus.

As best we can make out, after Mark had written his account, Matthew and Luke saw it, or a copy of it, and decided to do their own versions of the life of Jesus. From careful study we know that they had both Mark's account and another collection of information about Jesus. This second collection is called "Q" from the German word for source. It is relatively easy to see how Matthew and Luke used both Mark and Q in putting together the accounts.

Similarities between these three Gospels was observed and commented upon very early, but it was not until 1774 that a scholar named   J. J. Griesbach published a synopsis of the Gospels of Matthew, Mark, and Luke so that they could be seen together. He laid them out side by side and made it easy to see where they were exactly alike, or nearly alike, or where they differed. From that time on these Gospels have been called the "Synoptic Gospels."

	Peculiarities	Coincidences
Mark	7%	93%
Matthew	42%	58%
Luke	59%	41%
John	92%	8%

As you can see, John is markedly different from the other three. We will see why later.

We feel that Mark wrote from his own memory, despite the fact that he was not a long-term disciple. He also apparently used his recollection of the preaching of Paul, of Barnabus, and   of Peter, as well as the oral tradition from the living witnessess around him.

Matthew used his own memory, Mark's account, the Q collection, and the oral tradition.

Luke used Mark's account, the Q collection, mental or written notes from Paul's preaching and other early preachers, and the oral tradition.

Mark's, Matthew's, and Luke's purposes in writing about Jesus were different, so their narratives were given different perspectives. Mark wanted to present the good news to all citizens of the Roman Empire. Matthew wanted to present Jesus as the fulfillment of messianic prophecies and as a savior not of Jews alone but also of the gentiles. Luke wanted to present Jesus as a brother to all human kind and to make his life and teaching attractive and understandable to first-century Greek culture; he seems also to have had a special interest in making the gospel attractive to women.

Mark

This is the oldest of the Gospels. It was probably written in Rome before the destruction of the temple in Jerusalem in 70 A.D. We are reasonably certain that Mark wrote this Gospel at the direction of Peter, the apostle. Some quotes from the early Church Fathers give ground to this. Papius, who wrote around 130-150 A.D., says "Mark was Peter's interpreter and wrote accurately all Peter said." Clement of Alexandria (150-220) said that Peter preached to the nobility in Rome and that Mark wrote at their request this Gospel in order that they could commit to memory what Peter said.

We know a good bit about Mark from the Gospels, the Book of Acts and other sources. He came from a home within the city walls of Jerusalem, and his father had died. His home was a favorite meeting place of the early church; when Herod began to persecute the members of the early church, Peter escaped and "made for the house of Mary, the mother of John Mark, where a large company was at prayer." [18]

Barnabus, the companion of Paul, was Mark's cousin, and there is some evidence that Mark's house was the scene of the Last Supper; Mark may have trailed the disciples to the garden of Gethsemane:

Among those following was a young man with nothing on but a linen cloth. They tried to seize him; but he slipped out of the linen cloth and ran away naked. [19]

------

[18] Acts 12:12.

[19] Mark 14:51-52.

If this was Mark, it makes him an eyewitness to the scene of Jesus at prayer, his betrayal, and capture.

Mark went on the first missionary journey with Paul and Barnabus.

Mark wrote for gentiles generally, and he probably addressed himself specifically to the Roman citizens he came to know while with Peter in Rome. This is indicated by the fact that he translated the Aramaic expressions of Jesus; Jews would not have needed that! Also, he gave explanations of Jewish customs like washing of feet, the day before the Sabbath, etc. Furthermore, the term "Law" (a technical term in the Jewish community) is not mentioned at all, quotes from the Old Testament are comparatively few, a Greek term was explained by using a Latin one, and the literary climax is when the Roman centurion says: "Truly this man was a son of God." [20]

Mark writes with a direct style, there are no wasted words; he begins slap bang with the ministry of Jesus, "Here begins the gospel of Jesus. . . ." [21] He gives only a passing reference to his baptism and temptation. Mark gives us the only account we have of a consecutive twelve hours in Jesu's life in 1:21-39.

It is instructive that Mark never mentions the birth of Jesus, virgin or otherwise, and if he was recording what Peter preached, and Paul too (who also says nothing of the birth in any of his letters), we might conclude that the early church found nothing significant in it.

One third of Mark's Gospel is devoted to the last week of Jesus' life. The earliest manuscripts conclude the Gospel with 16:8, but there are a number of "longer endings" that float around. Some are attached to the translation we are using.

Matthew

I feel that this Gospel was written by a Christian of Jewish background who found himself dissatisfied with the Gospel of Mark because it included so little of the teachings of Jesus. He used

---

[20] Mark 15:39.

[21] Mark 1:1.

Mark's written work along with a collection of "sayings" of Jesus collected by the disciple Matthew (Papias, one of the early Church Fathers, said, "Matthew collected the sayings of Jesus in the Hebrew tongue"), and the "Q" materials. With the leisure of some reflecting time, Matthew sat down with this mass of material, made a detailed outline, and then carefully set down an arranged gospel. Clearly, it was a teaching tool; the Gospel is arranged in five blocks of teaching material as follows:

Introduction: The Birth of the King, chapters 1-2
Lesson I: Chapters 3-7
    Narrative: (3-7) the king begins his work
    Teaching: (5-7) manifesto of the kingdom
Lesson II: Chapters 8-11:1
    Narrative: (9-9:34) the king's power revealed
    Teaching: (9:35-11:1) the king commissions his disciples
Lesson III Chapters 11:2-13:53
    Narrative: (11:2-12) the king faces opposition
    Teaching: (13:1-53) the king unfolds his kingdom
Lesson IV: Chapters 13:54-19:1
    Narrative: (13:54-17) the king faces crisis in Galilee
    Teaching: (18-19:1) the king teaches the relationship of citizens to the kingdom
Lesson V: Chapters 19:2-26:1
    Narrative: (19:2-22) the king faces the cross
    Teaching: (19:23-26:1) watch for the kingdom
Conclusion: Chapter 26:2-28: the final triumph of the king

In addition to this teaching outline, the author also uses techniques that will help people to remember. This was not a time when people wrote notes or copied material. You read or heard and then had to remember. So he uses a scheme of numbers, especially 3s and 7s, and organizes the material around these factors. The genealogy is in 3 blocks; there are 3 angelic visitations, 3 descriptions of Jesus' mission, 3 parables of sowing, 3 warnings, 3 prayers in Gethsemane, 3 denials of Peter, 3 questions of Pilate, and 3 women at the cross.

Thus, Matthew's Gospel was written as a teaching tool, using much of the disciple Matthew's written sayings, by a Jew from a

city in Asia Minor, possibly Antioch, in about 90 A.D. His purpose
was to show that Jesus was the Messiah and fulfilled the ancient
expectations. For this reason he quotes extensively from the Old
Testament.

His other big point concerns the kingdom and the Church. One
of his teaching emphases is about discipleship. He alone, of all
Gospel writers, has a concern for the life of the Church, something
that appears on almost every page.

The author's own title to his work is the nucleus about which
the entire book revolves, "A table of the descent of Jesus Christ,
son of David, son of Abraham. . . ." [22]

There are so many places where Matthew reports teachings of
Jesus that are not found in the other Gospels that it is hard for me
to select just one to give you a taste of his writing. The one that
follows is representative:

> When he saw the crowds he went up the hill. There
> he took his seat, and when his disciples had gathered
> round him he began to address them. And this is the
> teaching he gave:
>> How blest are these who know their need of God;
>> the kingdom of Heaven is theirs.
>> How blest are the sorrowful; they shall find
>> consolation.
>> How blest are those of a gentle spirit; they shall
>> have the earth for their possession.
>> How blest are those who hunger and thirst to see
>> right prevail; they shall be satisfied.
>> How blest are those who show mercy; mercy shall
>> be shown to them.
>> How blest are those whose hearts are pure;   they
>> shall see God.
>> How blest are the peacemakers; God shall call them
>> his sons.
>> How blest are those who have suffered persecution
>> for the cause of right; the kingdom of Heaven is
>> theirs.

---

[22] Matthew 1:1.

How blest you are, when you suffer insults and
persecution and every kind of calumny for my sake.
Accept it with gladness and exultation, for you have
a rich reward in heaven; in the same way they
persecuted the prophets before you. [23]

Luke

Matthew may be seen as having written a second edition of
Mark, but Luke was writing a new book at about the same time, 90
A.D. Luke certainly used Mark, but not necessarily as a guide.
While I like Mark for his vigor and straightforward writing, I like
Luke for his sensitivity. We know that Luke was not a Jew; he was
the only non-Jew to write part of the New Testament, as far as we
know. He was a physician by training, and he was well-schooled in
language; his Greek is the best in the New Testament.
Luke wrote with an historians care; for example, he gives us six
different sources for the dating of the appearance of John the
Baptist in 3:1-2. Luke's purpose was to present the founder and the
founding of "the way" to gentiles, and he does it with great
sensitivity.
His sensitivity toward women can be demonstrated in a number
of ways. For example, the birth scene is told from a woman's point
of view, and Luke tells of Elizabeth and her encouragement of Mary.
Luke also treats women sympathetically in the story of the widow of
Nain, the story of Anna, the description of the anointing of Jesus
feet, and in the stories of Mary and Martha and of Mary Magdalene.
Luke was also aware of the plight of the poor. He says that
Mary's offering was the offering of the poor, and it can also be
seen in his story of the rich man and Lazarus. Luke also translates
Jesus' words from the Sermon on the Mount:

How blest are you who are in need. . . . How blest are
you who now go hungry. . . . But alas for you who are

---

[23] Matthew 5:1-12.

rich; you have had your time of happiness. . . . Alas for
you who are well-fed now; for you shall go hungry. [24]

Luke was also sensitive to the position of the underdog as seen
in his stories of Zacchaeus the tax collector, of the prodigal son,
and of the penitent thief.

Furthermore, he showed sympathy toward all people everywhere
in his claim that salvation is for all, without distinction, and in his
stories of the Samaritan (called good), of the grateful leper who was
also a Samaritan, and the Roman centurion.

Whereas the other synoptic gospels quote Isaiah 40 in connection with Jesus' ministry partially: "Prepare a way for the Lord;
clear a straight path for him, . . ." Luke alone adds the rest of the
statement: "and all mankind shall see God's deliverance." From then
on it is clear that Luke sees all persons in the salvation picture.

Luke's is a Gospel of good news, healing, and liberation for all.
Here is a unique Luke piece:

> But [the lawyer] wanted to vindicate himself, so he
> said to Jesus, "And who is my neighbor?" Jesus replied,
> "A man was on his way from Jerusalem down to Jericho
> when he fell in with robbers, who stripped him, beat him,
> and went off leaving him half dead. It so happened that
> a priest was going down by the same road; but when he
> saw him, he went past on the other side. So too a Levite
> came to the place, and when he saw him went past on the
> other side. But a Samaritan who was making the journey
> came upon him, and when he saw him was moved to pity.
> He went up and bandaged his wounds, bathing them with
> oil and wine. Then he lifted him on to his own beast,
> brought him to an inn, and looked after him there. Next
> day he produced two silver pieces and gave them to the
> innkeeper, and said, 'Look after him; and if you spend any
> more, I will repay you on my way back.' Which of these
> three do you think was neighbor to the man who fell into
> the hands of the robbers?" He answered, The one who

---

[24] Luke 6: 20-25.

showed him kindness. Jesus said, "Go and do as he did." [25]

Luke also wrote a second volume, called Acts, which we shall consider later.

John

With John we come to a serious problem. This book makes radical departures from the first three gospels. We do not know who wrote it, but it was probably written in Ephesus around 100 A.D. It is less historical and more spiritual than the others, and was written with people of a Greek culture in mind.

The purpose is stated not at the beginning but at the end:

> There were indeed many other signs that Jesus performed in the presence of his disciples, which are not recorded in this book. Those here written have been recorded in order that you may hold the faith that Jesus is the Christ, the Son of God, and that through this faith you may possess life by his name. [26]

Perhaps it was written for catechumens (those seeking membership in the Church).

There are striking differences in this Gospel in such matters as the time of the cleansing of the temple (John puts it at the beginning of Jesus public ministry, while in Mark it comes at the end) and the time of the Last Supper and crucifixion (John has Jesus crucified before Passover, Mark afterward).

But that is not the point. The author's stated purpose was not historical accuracy; rather he has selected certain "signs" that the reader or hearer might believe. He was not interested in giving a chronological account of the life of Jesus; he was interested in witnessing to certain signs and teachings that would lead to belief

---

[25] Luke 10:29-37.

[26] John 20:30-31.

that this Jesus was the Messiah. The events that he chooses to write about usually conclude with an affirmation of belief or disbelief. In this respect the climax of the Gospel is the incident of the appearance of the risen Christ to the disciple Thomas:

> Then he said to Thomas, "Reach your finger here; see my hands. Reach your hand here and put it into my side. Be unbelieving no longer, but believe." And Thomas said, "My Lord and my God!" 27

Much of John is unique. Remember the chart that showed that 92 percent of the writing is NOT contained in Matthew, Mark, or Luke. In addition there is one fact that is very important for our theology derived from the New Testament writings. The Greek word, *agape* which is translated "love" is a special word to denote a selfless love, a love that gives and expects nothing in return, a love that lives for others. Paul uses the word to define the special gift he speaks of in I Corinthians 13. But the writer of John's Gospel uses that word more than any of the others.

	Matthew	Mark	Luke	John	I John
No. of Times *agape* is used	9	6	14	44	46

It is almost impossible in a brief space to select a passage to give the flavor of John, but here is one that I call the Magnificent Overture:

> When all things began, the Word already was. The Word dwelt with God, and what God was, the Word was. The Word, then, was with God at the beginning, and through him all things came to be; no single thing was created without him. All that came to be was alive with his life, and that life was the light of men. The light shines on in the dark, and the darkness has never mastered it. 28

---

27 John 20:26-28.

28 John 1:1-5.

Chapter 9

Acts of the Apostles

With Acts we move to another type of literature. This is the only book that can be called history in the New Testament. Like all history books, this is one person's account of events. No historian can write everything, so here Luke picks and chooses what to include and what to omit.

This is the only authentic history of the early church from its birth at Pentecost in 30 A.D. to about 60 A.D. And what a time it was; doctrines were being crystallized, organization was being developed, and policies were being set for the future.

This book also gives us insight into sermonic methods of the early church as well as views of social, economic, and moral conditions of great cities like Antioch, Corinth, and Jerusalem.

Luke gives his purpose in the opening sentences:

> In the first part of my work, Theophilus, I wrote all that Jesus did and taught from the beginning until the day when, after giving instruction through the Holy Spirit to the apostles whom he had chosen, he was taken up to heaven. [29]

He then launches into what happened next.

Acts is written from the point of view of a predominantly non-Jewish church already interested in its origins. It tries to explain how this Jewish-inspired religion became so popular, why members are baptized "in the name of Christ," why holding things in common is important, the origin of the Lord's Supper, how came deacons, how did Jews first preach to gentiles, etc.

But the overriding purpose of Luke's work appears to be to show to important persons the amazing spread of Christianity from Jerusalem to Rome. There is a dramatic series of accounts and

---

[29] Acts 1:1-2.

summaries in the work. Scholars have divided Luke's book in several ways. Here is one that I find helpful:

Chapters 1:1-6:7 tells of the church in Jerusalem and Peters preaching.
> Summary: The word of God now spread more and more widely;   the number of disciples in Jerusalem went on increasing   rapidly, and very many of the priests adhered to the Faith.

Chapters 6:8-9:31 describes the spread of Christianity through Palestine and the martyrdom of Stephen.
> Summary: Meanwhile the church, throughout Judea, Galilee, and Samaria, was left in peace to build up its strength. In the fear of the Lord, upheld by the Holy Spirit, it held on its way and grew in numbers.

Chapters 9:32-12:24 covers the conversion of Paul and the Church being established in Asia Minor.
> Summary: Meanwhile the word of God continued to grow and spread.

Chapters 12:25-16:5 tells of the continued spread of the church in Asia Minor and the preaching tour of Galatia.
> Summary: And so, day by day, the congregations grew stronger in faith and increased in numbers.

Chapters 16:6-19:20 relates the extension of the church to Europe and the work of Paul in Corinth and Ephesus.
> Summary: In such ways the word of the Lord showed its power, spreading more and more widely and effectively.

Chapters 19:21-28:31 tells of the arrival of Paul in Rome and his imprisonment.
> Summary: He stayed there two full years at his own expense, with a welcome for all who came to him, proclaiming the kingdom of God and teaching the facts about the Lord Jesus Christ quite openly and without hinderance.

Oh, how I wished Luke had written Volume III.

One of the startling things about this work of history is the way it differs from the epistles. There, you will remember, we saw the account of violent controversies that marked the early days of the Church. Luke does not mention them. Only Paul's letters to the Corinthian church, for instance, give us the scene of those stormy first years; you do not find it mentioned in Acts.

Luke also records for us two important "speeches." Whether these are verbatim or just concepts does not matter so much. It does give us an indication of what Peter and Paul felt was important. The first of these is Peter's speech in Jerusalem:

> Then Peter, filled with the Holy Spirit, answered, "Rulers of the people and elders, if the question put to us today is about help given to a sick man, and we are asked by what means he was cured, here is the answer, for all of you and for all the people of Israel: it was by the name of Jesus Christ of Nazareth, whom you crucified, whom God raised from the dead; it is by his name that this man stands here before you fit and well. This Jesus is the stone, rejected by the builders, which has become the keystone--and you are the builders. There is no salvation in anyone else at all, for there is no other name under heaven granted to men, by which we may receive salvation. [30]

The speech of Paul in Acts 13 is longer and more involved. But the thing that bothers me most about these and other speeches in Acts is that if they truly reflect what the apostles said, then they were more interested in teaching about Jesus than teaching what Jesus taught about the way of life called love.

---

[30] Acts 4:8-12.

Chapter 10

Literature of Persecution

We must focus on what was happening in Rome itself to understand the next writing in the New Testament. Let me begin with Augustus Caesar. By 31 B.C. he had successfully brought order out of the long civil war in the Roman Empire which had gone on for at least a century. The Empire was ready for peace, and Augustus brought peace that lasted for two centuries and included the entire Mediterranean world.

In 14 A. D. Augustus was succeeded by Tiberius. The time period from this event until the death of Marcus Aurelius in 180 A. D. is known as the Great Age of the Roman Empire. Tiberius was an excellent administrator, but the most important event in world history which took place in the Empire during his rule was the trial and execution of Jesus in Jerusalem. Its significance was so little understood at the time that it passed unnoticed by imperial chroniclers until Christianity gained recognition under Constantine in the fourth century. The list of persons that concern us follows:

Gaius Caligula (37-41 A.D.) became insane, regarded himself as a god, and was assassinated.

Claudius (41-54 A.D.) created a permanent bureaucracy for civil administration (woe for the future).

Nero (54-68 A.D.) studied with the philosopher Seneca, but he soon gave up that kind of training. His private life was filled with scandalous behavior. In 64 A.D. a great fire began in the shops of the east end of the Circus and burned ten of the fourteen wards of the city. Though he hastened to take proper relief measures, it was said that during the fire he sat in his palace on the Palatine, played his lyre, and recited verses. The city was rebuilt with wider streets and of better materials, but Nero reserved a large area between the Palatine and the

Esquiline for a park and an imperial palace, the Golden House, beautifully designed and decorated. This led to the accusation that Nero had started the fire in order to clear the land and get his palace (the first inner city redevelopment?). He looked for a scapegoat and found it in an obscure sect called Christians. These unfortunates were convicted of arson and put to death in most horrible ways to satisfy public clamor. The years that followed were filled with terror. To obtain money to pay for the rebuilding of the city and provide for his own extravagances, Nero revived the law of treason, struck down many wealthy senators on trumped-up charges in order to confiscate their estates.

Vespasian (69-79 A.D.) rebuilt the city and built the Colosseum on part of Nero's park.

Titus (79-81 A.D.) destroyed Jerusalem in quelling the rebellion there in 70 A.D. He is known primarily for a famous catastrophe that took place during his reign, the eruption of Vesuvius, which buried the city of Pompeii.

Domitian (81-96 A.D.) was a real right-wing conservative and revived old practices in morals and religion. During his reign, scandalous actions and writing were suppressed and a vestal virgin who had broken her vows was buried alive according to ancient law. Attempts to restore the old religion brought the Christians to his attention and brought persecutions throughout the empire. Christians in Rome during Nero's time were punished as incendiaries, not as Christians, but Domitian's religiosity led him to punish and execute them on charges of violating the law by belonging to associations for an unlicensed religion, by holding secret meetings, and by offending the majesty of the emperor. Domitian was assassinated in 96 A.D., and by order of the Senate his name was erased from his monuments and his memory forever cursed.

Aware of all this going on in the Roman Empire, and knowing that the emperor was demanding to be worshiped as divine, we are ready to look at three sections of the New Testament: Hebrews,

Revelation, and I Peter. They were all written in times of persecution or as reflections upon such times, probably during the reign of Domitian (81-96 A.D.).

Hebrews

We often hear this portion of the New Testament referred to as the "Epistle to the Hebrews" or "Letter to the Hebrews," but it is really not a letter at all. It is more a written sermon. Usual conjecture is that it was written by someone who knew the group to whom it was going, but could not be present to speak it, so he wrote it. It clearly was written to encourage a group facing persecution. Perhaps some had already wavered, or had even already returned to the established, traditional faith of Moses. We do not know who wrote it, to whom it was written, or when it was written, though, various early scholars have identified the following as possible writers: Apollos, Aquila, Priscilla, Luke, and even Clement (who lived much later).

Hebrews contains long arguments to prove the superiority of Jesus over all possible rivals, including Moses and angels. It contains what we would call philosophic arguments.

These people to whom the sermon was written were obviously not weaklings; they had already lost property and been severely persecuted. So the best parts are not the ones that try to establish Jesus' place as the great high priest, but the ones that bluntly say, have courage and hold fast:

And what is faith? Faith gives substance to our hopes, and makes us certain of realities we do not see.
It is for their faith that the men of old stand on record.
By faith Abraham obeyed the call to go out to a land destined for himself and his heirs, and left home without knowing where he was to go. By faith he settled as an alien in the land promised him, living in tents, as did isaac and Jacob, who were heirs to the same promise. For he was looking forward to the city with firm foundations, whose architect and builder is God.

> By faith even Sarah herself received strength to conceive, through she was past the age. . . .
> All these persons died in faith. They were not yet in possession of the things promised, but had seen them far ahead and hailed them, and confessed themselves no more than strangers or passing travelers on earth. . . .

There follows the roll call of Isaac, Moses, Rahab, Gideon, Barak, Samson, David, Samuel, and others, and then continues:

> Through faith they overthrew kingdoms, established justice, saw God's promises fulfilled. They muzzled raving lions, quenched the fury of fire, escaped death by the sword. Their weakness was turned to strength, they grew powerful in war, they put foreign armies to rout. Women received back their dead raised to life. Others were tortured to death, disdaining release, to win a better resurrection. Others again, had to face jeers and flogging, even fetters and prison bars. They were stoned, they were sawn in two, they were put to the sword, they went about dressed in skins of sheep or goats, in poverty, distress, and misery. They were too good for a world like this. They were refugees in deserts and on the hills, hiding in caves and holes in the ground. These also, one and all, are commemorated for their faith. . . .
> And what of ourselves? With all these witnesses to faith around us like a cloud, we must throw off every encumbrance, every sin to which we cling, and run with resolution the race for which we are entered, our eyes fixed on Jesus, on whom faith depends from start to finish: Jesus who, for the sake of the joy that lay ahead of him, endured the cross, making light of its disgrace, and has taken his seat at the right hand of the throne of God. [31]

What powerful writing. It is read today by persons in all sorts of oppressed conditions. It still gives hope and courage to those willing to take the risk of faith.

---

[31] Hebrews 11, selected verses.

Revelation

We come now to a book of the New Testament that has provided religious nuts with much material. It is too bad really, for this book shows tremendous creative writing, and I often present it as a drama, complete with prologue, seven acts, and an epilogue.

First off, let us call it by its proper name, Revelation, NOT Revelation*s*. The proper title sets it in its proper literary genre, for "revelation" means apocalyptic. Remember from the introduction that there are several other books that fit this grouping: Daniel in the Old Testament and Enoch in the Apocrypha.

This drama was written during the time of Domitian, who really made a thing of his "divinity," insisting that all persons worship him. He felt that the way to unite the empire was to reassert the pledge affirming that Domitian is lord, or you die. Obviously the Christians could not do that. They said, "Jesus is lord" which carried the corollary, "Caesar is not lord."

The persecution that occurred over this was widespread. Most people in the empire thought little of taking this loyalty oath, but a small group, the Jews and the Christians, absolutely refused. They were cited as unpatriotic and subversive and they were jailed, tortured, and killed for their refusal to give the emperor what he wanted.

Once again, as with Hebrews, we do not know who wrote Revelation, where it was written, or the exact date of its composition. We do feel rather certain it was written for broad distribution, which is what it got.

The book has three main divisions:

Seven "letters" to the churches of Asia Minor, chapters 1-4;

A series of visions (some pretty wild, as in Ezekiel), chapters 5-11; and

The story of the war between the Devil and the Lamb with the concluding vision of the Final Judgment and of the New World from which evil and suffering have been abolished.

It is important to put yourself into the mental framework of the author and his day to understand this work. Here is a creative person, committed to Jesus as the Christ and witnessing the persecution and what must have looked like the extinction of the Church. So he writes a dramatic, powerful piece to give courage. The book has a message that is delivered with matchless force: Kings have no power over you, violence cannot destroy you; spiritual power is what endures, and material force cannot destroy it; evil could not destroy Jesus, and it cannot destroy you, for you belong to him; victory is not to the empire and its soldiers, but to sacrificial love. The conclusion is one that we can be thankful for every day. It is a vision, a remarkable vision:

> Then I saw a new heaven and a new earth. . . . I saw the holy city, new Jerusalem, coming down out of heaven from God. . . .
> Then he showed me the river of the water of life, sparkling like crystal, flowing from the throne of God and of the Lamb down the middle of the city's street. On either side of the river stood a tree of life, which yields twelve crops of fruit, one for each month of the year; the leaves of the trees serve for the healing of the nations. Every accursed thing shall disappear. The throne of God and of the Lamb will be there, and his servants shall worship him; they shall see him face to face, and bear his name on their foreheads. There shall be no more night, nor will they need the light of lamp or sun, for the Lord God will give them light; and they shall reign for evermore. [32]

And then a promise:

> "Come!" say the Spirit and the bride. "Come!" let each

---

[32] Revelation 21:1-2, 22:1-5.

hearer reply. Come forward, you who are thirsty; accept the water of life, a free gift to all who desire it. [33]

I Peter

Once again, we do not know who wrote this book or where. It seems clear it was intended for circulation in Asia Minor and I feel it belongs to the same basic period of persecution as the others we have dealt with here. Many consider it a "gentle" letter and some think it was a baptismal sermon. Certainly it was a tract for the times.

Those times were hard:

> My dear friends, do not be bewildered by the fiery ordeal that is upon you, as though it were something extra-ordinary. It gives you a share in Christ's sufferings, and that is cause for joy. [34]

There is a marvelous understatement here: ". . . even though now you smart for a little while . . ." [35] many would be killed!

But the key word is hope and to these persecuted Christians the author writes encouragement:

> But you are a chosen race, a royal priesthood, a dedicated nation, and a people claimed by God for his own, to proclaim the triumphs of him who has called you out of darkness into his marvelous light. You are now the people of God, who once were not his people; outside his mercy once, you have now received his mercy. [36]

---

[33] Revelation 22:17.

[34] I Peter 4:12-13.

[35] I Peter 1:3.

[36] I Peter 2:9-10.

Chapter 11

The Pastoral Epistles

The three letters, I and II Timothy and Titus, are called the pastoral epistles because they were written to pastors. They were not intended for general circulation as were most of the others nor for specific congregations.

There is much debate about who wrote them. I do not believe that Paul was the author. Why not?

The language is quite different from that of the earlier epistles, though of course Paul could have had a secretary in his old age who used his language rather than that of Paul himself.

The concepts expressed in the Epistles are not the same as in the other letters, especially the concept of faith. Paul held faith to be courageous and confident acceptance of Jesus as Christ, but the Epistles define it as the holding of opinions about Jesus.

Most important is that there is no room in the Paul's life as described by Luke in Acts to fit in activities that these letter indicate, for instance, a journey to Crete.

However, these letters do give us a good glimpse of life in the early Church, a little later than in Acts. The church as discussed in these epistles has developed into an institution and has a hierarchy of pastors and bishops. Further, they tell second generation Christians how they ought to live. In this respect these letters should be grouped with some of those writings I spoke of early on, such books as *The Teaching of the Twelve Apostles.*

I and II Timothy

These letters were written to Timothy, who was in charge of the congregation at Ephesus. In the first letter, he is warned about the heretics who are perverting the Gospel, told how worship should be carried out, and given the duties of bishops and deacons. In the second letter, a much more intimate one, Timothy is encouraged to stand fast in the face of error in the church and persecution outside. There is an especially poignant section in which the writer shows his own lonelines:

> As for me, already my life is being poured out on the altar, and the hour for my departure is upon me. I have run the great race, I have finished the course, I have kept faith. And now the prize awaits me, the garland of righteousness which the Lord, the all-just Judge, will award me on that great Day; and it is not for me alone, but for all who have set their hearts on his coming appearance. [37]

Titus

This letter was written to the person in charge of the congregation in Crete. It is very much like I Timothy.

---

[37] II Timothy 4:6-8.

Chapter 12

Other New Testament Books

James

I like this book. Luther did not. Luther did not like it because it emphasizes the need to do something in order to have faith. "Faith without works is dead," said James bluntly. Luther found this troublesome because his fight was with the Roman Catholic church of his day which said that all you have to do to gain salvation is good works. Luther said all you have to have is faith and faith alone. So he called this book an "epistle of straw" and wanted it thrown out of the New Testament.

Well, it certainly is a practical book. It deals with very concrete situations like:

Don't show snobbery in worship:

> My brothers, believing as you do in our Lord Jesus Christ, who reigns in glory, you must never show snobbery. For instance, two visitors may enter your place of worship, one a well-dressed man with gold rings, and the other a poor man in shabby clothes. Suppose you pay special attention to the well-dressed man and say to him, "Please take this seat," while to the poor man you say, "You can stand; or you may sit here on the floor by my foot-stool," so you not see that you are inconsistent and judge by false standards? [38]

Don't be a hypocrite:

_____

[38] James 2:1-4.

My brothers, what use is it for a man to say he has faith when he does nothing to show it? Can that faith save him? Suppose a brother or a sister is in rags with not enough food for the day, and one of you says, "Good luck to you, keep yourselves warm, and have plenty to eat," but does nothing to supply their bodily needs, what is the good of that? So with faith; if it does not lead to action, it is in itself a lifeless thing. [39]

Watch your tongue:

All of us often go wrong; the man who never says a wrong thing is a perfect character, able to bridle his whole being. If we put bits into horses' mouths to make them obey our will, we can direct their whole body. Or think of ships: large they may be, yet even when driven by stormy gales they can be directed by a tiny rudder on whatever course the helmsman chooses. So with the tongue. It is a small member but it can make huge claims.

What an immense stack of timber can be set ablaze by the tiniest spark! And the tongue is, in effect, a fire. It represents among our members the world with all its wickedness; it pollutes our whole being; it keeps the wheel of our existence red-hot, and its flames are fed by hell. [40]

The problem of great possessions:

Next a word to you who have great possessions. Weep and wail over the miserable fate descending on you. Your riches have rotted; your fine clothes are moth-eaten; your silver and gold have rusted away, and their very rust will be evidence against you and consume your flesh like fire. You have piled up wealth in an age that is near its close. The wages you never paid to the men who mowed

---

[39] James 2:14-17.

[40] James 3:2-6.

your fields are loud against you, and the outcry of the reapers has reached the ears of the Lord of Hosts. You have lived on earth in wanton luxury, fattening yourselves like cattle--and the day for slaughter has come. [41]

We do not know for sure who wrote it, but we are reasonably certain it was written rather early, perhaps around 60 A.D. Tradition says that James, the brother of Jesus, wrote it and there is nothing to mitigate against that view. William Barkley makes a good case for this. He points out that James, during Jesus' ministry, was a detractor but we know that after the resurrection James was one of the chief leaders of the new church in Jerusalem. Barkley notes that in I Corinthians 15, where Paul is giving a list of the resurrection appearances of Jesus, he says, "After that, he was seen by James," and conjectures that Jesus wanted especially to include James, to win him over, and he did.

As in the Old Testament, many of the writers of the New Testament had their favorite "word" or thought. Paul's was faith, Peter's was hope, John's was love, and James' word was wisdom.

I, II and III John

The first of these is more a homily than a letter, but the second and third are in the form of a letter. I am inclined to believe that the apostle John wrote them late in his long life. They show remarkably mature judgment, and they pass on to the second and third generation Christians some sage advice. John seems upset at the complacency of these Christians. Note that there is little or no reference to persecution. Things have calmed down. As a matter of fact it is too calm and too casual. We can date these writings to around 100 A.D.

I like I John, for his "word" is love. He gives us that very simple, yet profound definition of God: "God is love," that is, agape love. Agape love is that which gives and expects nothing in return, a love that lives for others. Then he gives us a real whammy. The enormity of the statement is often lost, so we need to carefully listen:

---

[41] James 5:1-5.

Dear friends, let us love one another, because love is from God. Everyone who loves is a child of God and knows God, but the unloving know nothing of God. . . . If God thus loved us . . . we in turn are bound to love one another. Though God has never been seen by any man, God himself dwells in us if we love one another; his love is brought to perfection within us . . . [now watch out!] . . . God is love; he who dwells in love is dwelling in God, and God in him. . . . There is no room for fear in love; perfect love banishes fear. . . . We love because he loved us first. But if a man says, "I love God," while hating his brother, he is a liar. If he does not love the brother whom he has seen, it cannot be that he loves God whom he has not seen. And indeed this command comes to us from Christ himself: that he who loves God must also love his brother. [42]

Jude

You probably have heard very little of this little book of the New Testament. It is only twenty-five verses long. We do not know who wrote it, but it was intended as a circular letter. It was written very late, well after 100 A.D., and it has one theme: Shape up morally.

Jude had a lot of trouble getting into the New Testament at all, and there is still a great deal of discomfort about its inclusion.

II Peter

Here we have the same situation as Jude. This piece is longer, but (another parallel) it condemns false teachers who try to excuse immoral behavior. It was written after Jude and includes much of Jude in its text. It may have been written as late as 150 A.D.

---

[42] I John 4, selected verses.

Part III

The Apocrypha

Chapter 13

Introduction to the Apocrypha

We come now to the third part of the Bible. In a real sense this section will be the newest to Protestants, for we have generally been denied access to the Apocrypha, yet it provides very important insights to the time of Jesus.

The term apocrypha is used in several ways by different religious groups. It comes from a Greek word meaning "hidden away" or "secret." It was applied at first to works not considered suitable for general circulation. There are three words we need to examine now.

APOCRYPHA has been used in the Christian church to designate the collection of books which, while acknowledged to have a certain value and interest, were not recognized as part of the Bible. They were not found in the Hebrew Scriptures, but were part of the Greek translation of the Hebrew Scriptures done in Alexandria, Egypt, and called the Septuagint. They later appeared in Latin when Jerome did his translation called the Vulgate.

The Roman Catholic Church accepted these books as being canonical (part of recognized scripture) at the Council of Trent in 1546 and refers to them as DEUTEROCANON-ICAL, meaning canonical books of a later date than the others.

PSEUDEPIGRAPHA is a term which is used for yet another set of books that were not originally included in either the Greek or Latin Bibles. The term implies that they were not written by those whose names they bear. Roman Catholics use the term apocrypha for these books.

Historical Interlude

Remember that around 539 B.C., Cyrus, the Persian king, ushered in a "world" empire and released the Jews from exile to return and rebuild the temple and Jerusalem. The books of Ezra and Nehemiah give us some details of the time. But in 332 B.C., Alexander the Great captured Jerusalem from the Persians (and then went on to take the rest of their empire too).

After Alexander died unexpectedly at the age of thirty-three, his empire was eventually divided among his generals. In little more than a decade the generals had become kings: Cassander in Macedon, Lysimachus in Thrace, Antigonus in Anatolia and Syria, Ptolemy in Egypt, and Seleucus in the East.

But seventy-year-old Antigonus wanted more, so he moved against Cassander. The others joined in to defeat Antigonus and carved up his kingdom so that Seleucus got Syria and Ptolemy got Palestine.

Even though Seleucus was assassinated as he stepped off his boat on the way to conquer Europe, the Seleucian Empire at its height claimed power over 30 million people of many nationalities, scattered over a million square miles of territory.

Finally (for our story), Antiochus III captured Palestine from the Ptolemys in 199 B.C., setting the scene for the Maccabean Revolt. Antiochus III increased the heavy taxes but otherwise treated the Jews rather well. However, his son, Antiochus IV, became zealous in attempting to force Greek culture on the people of the territory, especially those in Palestine. He built theatres and amphitheaters, stadiums and baths; in Jerusalem a gymnasium was constructed. (The word gymnasium is derived from the Greek word for naked, and such naked carrying on as went on in the gymnasia really antagonized the pious Jews.)

Antiochus IV came to think of Orthodox Jews as his enemies and sent an army to occupy Jerusalem and "Hellenize" it. He attacked the city on a Sabbath, knowing the Orthodox would not fight on that day. A fortress was built in Jerusalem and a program of forcing Greek culture on the inhabitants was instituted. Orders were given that Greek gods were to be worshipped; Jews were forbidden to observe the Sabbath, circumcision was prohibited, and copies of Hebrew scriptures were destroyed.

Finally, in December of 168 B.C., not only were sexual rites performed in the temple, but a pig was sacrificed on the altar of Yahweh, the "abomination of desolation" as it was referred to in Daniel 11:31. Furthermore, an elderly scribe was beaten to death for refusing to eat pork, and two mothers were thrown over the city wall because they had circumcised their newborn sons. Many other "abominable" things were done.

During this persecution, a priest named Mattathias stepped forth when a country man was about to desecrate the altar and slew him. He and his family fled northwest of Jerusalem to Modein and resolved to avenge the slaughter of the Jews. Judas, one of his sons, made it so difficult for the Seleucids that they called him Maccabeus, meaning "the hammer."

After about three years the Maccabeans were successful, retook Jerusalem, and cleansed the temple. It was decreed that "the rededication of the altar should be observed with joy and gladness at the same season each year," thereby starting the tradition of the Feast of Lights of Hanukkah. [1]

Judas Mattathias was killed in battle in 161 B.C. and though his brothers and others successfully defeated the Seleucids and gained independence for a while, they eventually got caught in the larger battle, the coming of the Roman Empire. Pompey, having conquered all Syria, moved on to take Jerusalem in 63 B.C. and not until the establishment of Israel in 1948 were the Jews again in control of any part of Palestine.

The literature we now consider came largely out of this period. There is common agreement that the date of writing of the following books is in the first and second century B.C., running from about 200 B.C. to 100 B.C.

---

[1] I Maccabees 4:59.

Chapter 14

Historical Writings

I Esdras

This book, probably written by a Jew from Alexandria, Egypt, about 150 B.C. tells the history of the Jews from about 621 to 444 B.C. It covers largely the same material as II Chronicles 35:1-36:23, all of Ezra, and Nehemiah 7:73-8:12.

In the Latin Bible, Ezra and Nehemiah are called I and II Esdras, and this book is called III Esdras.

I Maccabees

This is one of the important books of the Apocrypha. It is a straightforward telling of the history of the people during the Maccabean Revolt. It has an interesting beginning summarizing the fantastic worldwide exploits of Alexander the Great in nine verses:

> Alexander of Macedon, the son of Philip, marched from the land of Kittim, defeated Darius, king of Persia and Media, and seized his throne, being already king of Greece. In the course of many campaigns he captured fortified towns, slaughtered kings, traversed the earth to its remotest bounds, and plundered innumerable nations. When at last the world lay quiet under his rule, his pride knew no limits; he built up an extremely powerful army, and ruled over countries, nations, and dominions; all paid him tribute.
>
> The time came when he fell ill, and, knowing that he was dying, he summoned his generals, nobles who had been brought up with him from childhood, and divided his empire among them while he was still alive. Alexander

had reigned twelve years when he died. His generals took over the government, each in his own province. On his death they were all crowned as kings, and their descendants succeeded them for many years. They brought untold miseries upon the world. [2]

This book, probably written by a Jew in Jerusalem about 100 B.C., is our chief source of history for this important period of time before the birth of Jesus. It includes a detailed account of the battles and thoughts of the people from about 175 to 134 B.C.

II Maccabees

This book is essentially the same as I Maccabees, but it covers a shorter period of time (about fifteen years). The purpose of the author is religious instruction more than pure history. It was probably written in Greek in Egypt.

The author says that this work is a condensation of a five-volume history of Israel during the years 180-161 B.C.:

These five books of Jason I shall try to summarize in a single work; for I was struck by the mass of statistics and the difficulty which the bulk of the material causes to those wishing to grasp the narratives of this history. [3]

How I wish we had the five volumes so we could do our own condensing!

---

[2] I Maccabees 1:1-9.

[3] II Maccabees 2:23-24.

Chapter 15

Moralistic Novels

Tobit

This story could well be made into a pious soap opera on TV and run and rerun for quite some time. The theme is that God is with us even in the midst of trouble and suffering. To prove it we have not one but two characters who are innocent but have problems.

Tobit is the essence of the giving person, helpful to a fault. As a matter of fact it is because he did a good thing that he got his problem. He went out and retrieved a man who had died, and buried him. Since he touched a dead person he had become, by law, "unclean" and was not able to sleep in his own house. As he slept outside, close to the wall where birds were, some of their droppings fell on his eyes and he went blind.

The other character is Sarah. She also is pious and had the unfortunate experience of having been married seven times. Each husband died before the marriage could be consummated.

Tobits son, Tobias, sets out at his father's direction to seek a wife. The story of the trip is like a Norman Rockwell illustration complete with the pet dog trailing along. He finds Sarah and falls in love. Sarah's father, knowing her past history, goes out and digs a grave for Tobias while his mother prepares for the wedding. But everything works out happily in the end in this early version of the love boat.

Among other things in this story there is the negative form of the Golden Rule, "Do not do to anyone what you yourself would hate." [4]

There are also some admonitions like:

---

[4] Tobit 4:15.

Pay your workmen their wages the same day; do not make
any man wait for his money. [5]

Give food to the hungry and clothes to the naked.
Whatever you have beyond your own needs, give away to
the poor, and do not give grudgingly. [6]

Martin Luther says that this book offers a delicate, lovable, pious
comedy, with a God-fearing peasant or bourgeois suffering greatly in
his married life, but God always standing by to help and in the end
bringing him joy.

Judith

This book is a story of a feminist, "resistance" heroine who
saves the city of Bethulia and does in the commander of the
Assyrian army by cunning, without loosing her chastity.
The first seven chapters are a dull recitation of the events
leading up the main story. Holophernes, an Assyrian general, is
known for his ruthlessness. The city fathers of Bethulia, hearing of
his approach, are worried that he will defile the sacred temple and
do some other not-so-nice things. Holophernes decides to camp in
the valley, cut off the water and supplies, and wait until the
population gives up.
But Judith (her names means Jewess) decides to take matters
into her own hands. She is very beautiful, very devout, and very
crafty. After thirty-four days of seige, the people are complaining
and want to give up. Ozias, the mayor, says no, and urges his
people to trust God for five more days. Judith indignantly scolds
the mayor and the elders for attempting to force the hand of God.
Judith prays (it is a long prayer), then fixes herself up as if to
go to a party, including the packing of an overnight bag. She goes
out of the gate of the city, down into the valley, and approaches
the camp of the Assyrians. When challenged, she tells the Assyrian

[5] Tobit 4:14.

[6] Tobit 4:16.

guard that she is escaping the imminent fall of the city and that she will betray the whole population.

Holophernes buys her story and lets her stay. Each night she goes outside the camp with her basket of kosher food (she is very strict and law abiding) and prays so she will know when to tell Holopherenes the right moment to attack the city.

One night she is invited to a party in the camp. She dresses up for it and wins Holopherne's heart. He invites her to stay with him. She does, but he is so drunk that he goes to sleep before anything can happen.

At this point Judith takes his sword and cuts off his head. She puts the head in the basket and proceeds to go outside the camp, as she has done each of the other nights, so the guards are expecting her. But this time she goes back into the city of Bethulia. She shows the head declaring,

> though my face lured him to destruction, he committed no sin with me, and my honor is unblemished. [7]

The Jews attack the leaderless and panic-stricken enemy and drive them off forever.

> No one dared to threaten the Israelites again in Judith's lifetime, or for a long time after her death. [8]

Daniel and Susanna

Here is another story of a beautiful and pious Jewish woman! It is a detective story of sorts, a real Perry Mason.

This story starts out, as a good short story should, setting the scene with a few deft strokes:

> There once lived in Babylon a man named Joakim. He married Susanna, daughter of Hilkiah, a very beautiful and

---

[7] Judith 13:16.

[8] Judith 16:25.

devout woman. Her parents, religious people, had brought
up their daughter according to the law of Moses. Joakim
was very rich and his house had d a fine garden adjoining
it, which was a regular meeting-place for the Jews,
because he was the man of greatest distinction among
them. [9]

So it was one day that the judges and elders of the town were
holding court in the courtyard of Susanna. About noon their custom
was to depart, and the family then would come into their garden
and enjoy it. Susanna especially liked to come and walk about at
that time, and occasionally at least, to bathe in the pool.

Now it happened that two of the elders took special notice of
Susanna, and lusted after her. Neither was aware of the thoughts
of the other until one day, sneaking back into the garden after
court was over, they caught one another in lewd voyeurism. They
made a deal.

One very hot day they stayed and hid after court to watch
Susanna. She had her maids close the garden door for privacy and
leave her alone so she could bathe in the garden pool. The two
elders came out of hiding and told her if she did not lie with them
they would accuse her of being caught in the act with a young
man. She felt trapped knowing that the elders would be believed.
But she would not give in.

Susanna yelled for help, and the elders yelled for witnesses.
One ran and opened the garden door to the street. The servants
came. Susanna told her story, they told theirs. The next day she
was called before the judges and accussed. It looked bad for
Susanna. She was declared guilty and sentenced to death.

In comes the hero. As she is lead to her death, a young man
named Daniel comes mysteriously into the scene and demands to
cross-examine the witnesses. A new trial is held in the courtyard.
Daniel has the two elders removed and then calls in each one by
himself. He asked: "Under what tree did you see them together?"
One said under a clove tree, the other answered under the yew
tree. Daniel had them, and they got theirs.

---

[9] Daniel and Susanna 1:1-4.

And so an innocent life was saved that day. . . . And
from that day forward Daniel was a great man among
his people. [10]

This delightful story was very popular among both Jews and
early Christians.

Daniel, Bel, and the Snake

Like Susanna, this story is seen as an addition to the canonical
book of Daniel. Again Daniel is portrayed as a clever lawyer-type
who exposes deception.
The most popular god of the Babylonians was Bel (also known
as Marduk). He lived in one of the seven wonders of the ancient
world, an immense temple in Babylon. The king was obliged to give
vast quantities of food each day to feed this god and this was
placed in the temple. It was an obvious drain on the royal budget,
but the king went along with it. Daniel was asked why he didn't
worship this great god and he told the king bluntly it was because
the god was a dead thing, a phony. Listen to the narrative:

> So the king said to [Daniel], "Why do you not worship
> Bel?" [Daniel] replied, "Because I do not believe in
> man-made idols, but in the living God who created heaven
> and earth and is sovereign over all mankind." The king
> said, "Do you think that Bel is not a living god? Do you
> not see how much he eats and drinks each day?" Daniel
> laughed and said, "Do not be deceived, your majesty; this
> Bel of yours is only clay inside and bronze outside, and
> has never eaten anything." [11]

And the contest was on. The king put food in the temple and
had it sealed for the night. But the priests had a trap door under

---

[10] Daniel and Susanna 62-63.

[11] Daniel, Bel and the Snake 4-7.

the altar and a tunnel so they could get in and out unseen. Ah ha! But Daniel took the precaution of having fine ashes sifted over the floor before the temple was sealed for the night.

Next morning the seals were broken, the food was gone, the king was triumphant. Whoa, said Daniel. Look at the floor. There are footprints of men, women and children--your priests and their families! The king had them executed and Daniel got to destroy the image of Bel and the temple.

The second story tells of Daniel destroying a sacred dragon. He does this by feeding it cakes of pitch, fat, and hair. The people are enraged. Daniel is thrown into a lion's den (sound familiar?),- but is (again) untouched.

The author quickly makes his point that those who worship the true God, Yahweh, will be protected in every kind of trial.

Chapter 16

Two Teaching Pieces

The Wisdom of Solomon

It was common practice for the writers of "wisdom" literature to attach the name of Solomon to their works. Solomon obviously did not write all that has been attributed to him over the centuries, any more than George Washington slept in all those beds. The Wisdom of Solomon was probably written in Alexandria, Egypt, by a Jew well-versed in his own tradition and in the culture of the Greeks.

The purpose of this piece is to show that the wisdom of Yahweh is greater than the wisdom of the Egyptian or Greek gods, or of any other god for that matter.

> Hear then, you kings, take this to heart; learn your lesson, lords of the wide world; lend your ears, you rulers of the multitude, whose pride is the myriads of your people. It is the Lord who gave you your authority; your power comes from the Most High. He will put your actions to the test and scrutinize your intentions. Though you are viceroys of his kingly power, you have not been upright judges; you do not stand up for the law or guide your steps by the will of God. Swiftly and terribly will he descend upon you, for judgment falls relentlessly upon those in high place. [12]

---

[12] Wisdom of Solomon 6:1-5.

Ecclesiasticus, or The Wisdom of Jesus Son of Sirach

The point of this piece is the superiority of Hebrew wisdom. There is no real organization in this book; it is an unconnected series of proverb-type sayings on a wide range of subjects. It is, however, one of the more important books of the Apocrypha, and some of my favorite passages are quoted below.

On the glory of God in nature:

> Now I will call to mind the
>   works of the Lord
> and describe what I have seen;
> by the words of the Lord his works
>   are made.

> What a masterpiece is the clear
>   vault of the sky!
> How glorious is the spectacle of the heavens!
> The sun comes into view
>   proclaiming as it rises
>   how marvelous a thing it is,
>   made by the Most High.
> At noon it parches the earth,
>   and no one can endure its blazing heat.

> He made the moon also to serve
>   in its turn,
> a perpetual sign to mark the divisions of time.

> The brilliant stars are the beauty of the sky,
> a glittering array in the heights of the Lord.

> Look at the rainbow and praise its maker;
> it shines with a supreme beauty,
> rounding the sky with its gleaming arc,
> a bow bent by the hands of the Most High.

> His command speeds the snow-storm

and sends the swift lightning to execute his
sentence. [13]

In praise of illustrious heros of Israel's past, chapters 44-50 list
such personalities as Enoch, Noah, Abraham, Isaac, Joshua, David,
Josiah, and others.

About physicians:

> Honor the doctor for his services,
> for the Lord created him.
> His skill comes from the Most High,
> and he is rewarded by kings.
> The doctor's knowledge gives him high standing
> and wins him the admiration of the great.
> The Lord has created medicines from the earth,
> and a sensible man will not disparage them. [14]

Comments about marriage, 25:16-24.

On raising children, 30:12.

The first edition of Emily Post:

> If you are sitting at a grand table,
> do not lick your lips and exclaim,
>   "What a spread!"
> Remember, it is a vice to have a greedy eye.
>
> Do not reach for everything you see,
> or jostle your fellow-guest at the dish.
>
> Eat what is set before you like a gentleman;
> do not munch and make yourself objectionable.
> Be the first to stop for good manners sake

---

[13] Ecclesiasticus 42-43 (various selections).

[14] Ecclesiasticus 38:1-4.

and do not be insatiable,
or you will give offence. [15]

Advice to toastmasters:

If they choose you to preside at a
feast, do not put on airs;

Speak, if you are old--it is your privilege--
but come to the point and do not
interrupt the music.
Be brief, say much in few words,
like a man who knows and can still
hold his tongue. [16]

A marvelous piece about choice in life:

Do not say, "The Lord is to blame
for my failure";
it is for you to avoid doing what he hates.
Do not say, "It was he who led me astray";
he has no use for sinful men. . . .
When he made man in the beginning,
he left him free to take his own decisions;
if you choose, you can keep the commandments;
whether or not you keep faith is
yours to decide.
He has set before you fire and water;
reach out and take which you choose;
before man lie life and death,
and whichever he prefers is his. [17]

---

[15] Ecclesiasticus 31:12-17.

[16] Ecclesiasticus 32:1,3,8.

[17] Ecclesiasticus 15:11-17.

Chapter 17

A Devotional Piece

The Prayer of Manasseh

For the setting of this prayer we must go back to one of our historical interludes (page 43). Manasseh was one of the "bad" kings who followed "Good" King Hezekiah. He introduced and encouraged many foreign and pagan practices. For this he was punished by God. But II Chronicles gives us a sequel:

> Then Yahweh sent the generals of the king of Assyria against them, who captured Manasseh with hooks, put him in chains, and led him away to Babylon. In his distress he sought to appease Yahweh . . . humbling himself deeply . . . he prayed . . . and God relented at his prayer. [18]

This book purports to be the prayer that Manasseh made that day, but scholars feel that if it is, it was handed down orally and written very late. It found wide acceptance in the early church.

---

[18] II Chronicles 33:11-20.

Chapter 18

An Apocalyptic

II Esdras

    Remember that this type of (apocalyptic) literature is "an unveiling;" it stands with such others as the Book of Revelation. It is not just a straight telling of what the future might look like; rather it is told with symbols, some of them rather bizarre.

    This book deals agonizingly with the problems that have befallen the "chosen people" and discusses the justification of the anger and justice of God. It is really a tough one for modern people to understand.

    There is an interesting historical point about this book. A very prominent scholar of the fifteenth century, Pierre d'Ailly, published a collection of geographical essays. Among other things he believed that the earth was a sphere. He also took quite literally the writings of II Esdras and quoted several verses in his work:

> On the third day you ordered the waters to collect in a seventh part of the earth; the other six parts you made into dry land, and from it kept some to be sown and tilled for your service. . . . On the fifth day you commanded the seventh part, where the water was collected, to bring forth living things, birds and fishes. . . . You put them in separate places, for the seventh part where the water was collected was not big enough to hold them both. . . . To Leviathan you gave the seventh part, the water. [19]

---

[19] II Esdras 6:42, 47, 50, 52.

And now for the point. Christopher Columbus had a copy of this book in his library, and actually made margin markings in it. The erroneous statement from II Esdras about the small section of the earth that was water may well have helped Columbus decide that a voyage westward would not be all that far!

Chapter 19

Four Portions of Old Testament Books

The Rest of the Chapters of the Book of Esther

The title of this chapter tells it all, and the subtitle in *The New English Bible* includes "which are found neither in the Hebrew nor in the Syriac." Someone, perhaps the Greek translator in about 114 B.C., decided to add some material to the book of Esther. You will remember that that book, as popular as it was and is, never mentioned God. These additions do that and that is about all they do.

Baruch

This purports to have been written by Jeremiah's secretary, but it is actually from the "inter-testament" period. It was used by the early Church Fathers who said that the statements were quotes from Jeremiah. It is largely prayers, and may include some early hymns used in the synagogue services.

A Letter of Jeremiah

This is a rambling letter, not by Jeremiah, warning the people not to fall from the true faith and follow false idols.

The Song of the Three

The subtitle is "An addition in the Greek version of Daniel between 3.23 and 3.24." It is a supposed addition, along with Daniel and Susanna; and Daniel, Bel, and the Snake. It consists of a prayer by Azariah and a hymn sung by Daniel's three companions: Shadrach, Meshach, and Abednego. In *The Jerusalem Bible* this is found as a part of chapter 3. It is good to read it in this version to catch the rhythm of the antiphonal arrangement. It is a good piece to use in the liturgy.

Part IV

Conclusion

Chapter 20

Why These Books?

One of the most frequent questions I am asked is why we have only these particular books included in the Bible, when there were many many more written and in circulation. The answer lies in a discussion of what is called the canon.

The word "canon" is so complex that my unabridged dictionary takes nine inches to define it. It comes from various roots that mean "a measuring line, rule, model." In general, it is a list or a catalog. In ecclesiastical language, it is a list of books which are received as being genuine and inspired holy scripture. The story as to how these lists were put together is a long and stormy one.

The first thing to remember is that no writer in either testament (save Sirach, and his book was not accepted into the canon) thought of their writings as sacred scripture. Many other writings in both Old and New Testament times either did not survive, or survived but did not make it into the canon.

For the Old Testament, the process involved at least three major divisions and times. The Law, or the Pentateuch, was the first to be recognized as special. This happened around 400 B.C. These books were separated from other books and were considered to be the Law of Moses. From that time on, they could not be revised or enlarged, though some discrepancies did creep in due to copying, and still others came as they were translated into other languages.

The books known as the Prophets, called "former" and "later," with "former" dealing with the glories of Israel's past, and "later" giving a glimpse of the future, were not set apart as sacred until sometime between 200 B.C. and 30 A. D.

Finally the "Writings" were so designated by about 90 A.D. At this time there was a conference of rabbis who had sufficient prestige to make a list that held.

But there were other groups and other lists. On group now well known was the community at Qumran where the "Dead Sea

Scrolls" were found. Their list included some books unknown or rejected by the council at Jamnia in 90 A.D.

The collection out of Jamnia became known as the "Hebrew Bible" and was basically the edition known by Jesus and his disciples. It did not include the Apocrypha.

Another collection came from Alexandria, Egypt. It was the one translated into Greek and had a slightly different ordering of the books. It did include the Apocrypha. It was the collection used by Paul and the early church, for they were Greek-speaking people and needed this Greek translation. This edition was condemned in 130 A.D. by the Jewish council, but it was the edition that was used by Jerome in 384 A.D. when he translated the Old Testament into Latin. [1]

The story of the New Testament collection is similar. Again, none of the writers thought they were writing sacred scripture. As a matter of fact, by their time there was such a high tradition concerning the "Holy Scriptures" that I think it would have been a devastating thought to them. Their "scripture" was what we call the Old Testament.

Gradually the authority of the words that Jesus or the early apostles spoke was transferred to the written account of those words. Some of the liturgy (the prayers of the early church) began to mention the earliest Gospels as well as some of the writings of Paul and others as "scriptures."   Some writings of Clement and Justin Martyr (about 150 A.D.) mention both Old Testament and New Testament passages as "Scripture, Holy."

But it was not until Marcion came on the scene in 150 A.D. that a true list was circulated. He included Luke and ten letters of Paul. Other lists followed for many years, each different in content.

Finally, in 393 A.D., at a council held in Hippo in North Africa, and again at the Third Council of Carthage in 397 A.D., the present list of twenty-seven books was called "canonical."

At the time of the Reformation, this question was again opened. Martin Luther had particularly strong opinions as to what books should be in or out of the canon. He vehemently advocated

---

[1] See the table at the end of this chapter for a comparison of the listing of books between the "Protestant" Old Testament, The Hebrew Collection, and the Septuagint.

that the book of James, which he called an "epistle of straw," be removed. This whole question was of exceeding importance to the Reformers since they based their authority on Scripture alone as opposed to papal authority.

This also led to an almost fanatic attempt to publish only the most authentic translations of both Old and New Testaments. It also led to the rejection of the Apocrypha.

The Westminster Confession of Faith, written in 1643 by fallible human beings, all male and all clergy, found it necessary to list by name the books of both Old and New Testament that made up the canon.

> Under the name of Holy Scripture, or the Word of God written, are now contained all the books of the Old and New Testaments, which are these: . . . all of which are given by inspiration of God, to be the rule of faith and life. [2]

The document goes on to say:

> The books commonly called Apocrypha, not being of divine inspiration, are no part of the canon of the Scripture; and therefore are of no authority in the Church of God, nor to be any otherwise approved, or made use of, than other human writings. [3]

A Brief Word About an Explosive Subject: Authority

While my original intent was not to get into polemics in this book, I feel I must at least identify the "problem" of authority. Seldom do I teach this subject that I do not have someone wanting to argue this point. I put quotes around the word "problem," for it simply is not a problem to me and I cannot get excited about it. Yet I must admit that whole semesters are used in seminaries to talk

---

[2] *The Westminster Confession of Faith,* I, 2.

[3] *Ibid,* I, 3.

about it, books have been written about it, and I suppose various persons have drawn blood and signed covenants about it.

Let me give you my bias right up front. Among many little hymns and church ditties that I dislike is:

Jesus loves me this I know, for the Bible tells me so.

Now Jesus does love me. And this indeed I do know, but not because the Bible tells me so. Rather it is because some individual has reached out to me in a real way, or has touched me in a caring, unselfish way in a concrete experience in life, that I know God loves me. As I examine that experience I come to know that God loves me. I may go to the Bible to discover the source, or the resource, for doing it, but the Bible in and of itself will never convince me of much of anything about the nature of God, at least initially.

Certainly the pronouncement of some church council can not persuade me of the authority of the Bible, for I know too much of what went on in those councils of common, fallible human beings each advocating his own bias. They argued as to what should or should not be included, they threw books at each other, and they yelled until finally some pre-Presbyterian probably moved the "previous question" which effectively closed the debate and a vote was taken. We know from the history of the time that in some cases they went on to exile the losers. At least once, in the famous see-saw debate about the nature of Jesus, between Arius and Athenasius, the one lost at one council and was banished by the other, then the reverse happened at the next council, only to be followed by yet another reversal and exile! So much for feeling any loyalty about that process.

The Westminster Confession comes close to defining my position:

The authority of the Holy Scripture, for which it ought to be believed and obeyed, dependeth not upon the testimony of any man or church, but wholly upon God . . . the author thereof; and therefore it is to be received . . . yet, notwithstanding, our full persuasion and assurance of the infallible truth and divine authority thereof, is from

the inward work of the Holy Spirit, bearing witness by
and with the Word in our hearts. [4]

Table of Various Old Testament Book Listings

THE PROTESTANT	THE HEBREW	THE SEPTUAGINT
Law	*Torah*	*Laws*
Genesis	"In-beginning"	Genesis
Exodus	"These the names"	Exodus
Leviticus	"He called"	Leviticus
Numbers	"In the wilderness"	Numbers
Deuteronomy	"These the words"	Deuteronomy
History	*Former Prophets*	*Histories*
Joshua	Joshua	Joshua
Judges	Judges	Judges
Ruth	Samuel	Ruth
1&2 Samuel	1&2 Kings	1&2 Kingdoms
1&2 Kings		1&2 Paralipomena
1&2 Chronicles		
Ezra	*Later Prophets*	1 Esdras
Nehemiah	Isaiah	2 Esdras
Esther	Jeremiah	Esther
Esther	Ezekiel	Judith
	The Twelve	Tobit
	Hosea	1-4 Maccabees
	Joel	
Poetry	Amos	*Poetical Books*
Job	Obadiah	Psalms
Psalms	Jonah	Proverbs
Proverbs	Micah	Ecclesiastes
Ecclesiastes	Nahum	Song
Song of Solomon	Habakkuk	Job
	Zephaniah	Wisdom of Solomon
	Haggai	Wisdom of Jesus

---

[4] *Ibid.*, I, 4-5.

Major Prophets   Zechariah   Psalms of Solomon
Isaiah   Malachi
Jeremiah
Lamentations
Ezekiel
Daniel   *Writings*   *Prophetical Books*
                     Psalms   Hosea
Minor Prophets   Job   Amos
Hosea   Proverbs   Micah
Joel   Ruth   Joel
Amos   Song of Songs   Obadiah
Obadiah   Qoheleth   Jonah
Jonah   Lamentations   Nahum
Micah   Esther   Habakkuk
Nahum   Daniel   Zephaniah
Habakkuk   Ezra/Nehemiah   Haggai
Zephaniah   Chronicles   Zechariah
Malachi   Malachi
Habakkuk   Isaiah
Zephaniah   Jeremiah
Haggai   Baruch
Zechariah   Lamentations
Malachi   Letter of Jeremiah
                                            Ezekiel
                                            Daniel + additions

Chapter 21

Through the Looking Glass

A Sermon

There is a story told of a man who led the opening "exercises" at the church school. Every Sunday morning he would open the big pulpit Bible that was used on the lectern in the Sunday school assembly hall and read the lesson for the classes. He read the Bible with his eyes open but with his head closed.

Once he made the mistake of telling the children what he planned to read the next Sunday. Some of them got into the church the following Saturday, found the place where he would be reading in the Bible, and glued together some of the pages.

The next morning the man was piously reading one page of the big Bible, came to the bottom of the page where it said,

When Noah was 125 years old he took unto himself a wife, who was . . .

and here he turned the glued-together pages

140 cubits long, 40 cubits wide, built of gopher wood and covered with pitch inside and out.

He stopped, somewhat puzzled, and then read the passage again. Then he raised his eyes and said,

My friends, this is the first time I ever read that in the Bible, but I accept it as evidence of the assertion that we are fearfully and wonderfully made.

Now that is an example of how not to use the Bible. That is to make the mistake of looking AT the Bible and not THROUGH it

to see what is revealed there. It is like looking AT the dirty
window and seeing all the scratches and dirt of the winter instead
of looking THROUGH it to see the Spring scene beyond. It is like
listening to an old recording of Caruso and hearing only the surface
noise of imperfect recording and missing the great voice itself.

There are many people for whom the Bible does not seem to
have a message for our times. They tend to regard this book as
belonging to another age, to a totally different culture. Surrounded
and engulfed in the technological gadgetry of our contemporary
world, they seem unable to comprehend how Jewish peasants,
fishermen, shepherds, and kings of a bygone age could communicate
to them. They reject the suggestion that there is anything to be
gained by reading books written long ago by a Greek physician
ignorant of modern antibiotics, or that there is any profit from
reading a collection of letters written by a converted Pharisee
unacquainted with presentday theories of psychology.

But, except for the physical differences of a speeded-up
nuclear age, we are essentially no different from those who preceded
us by several thousand years. It is quite true that we have
invented many new machines, but we have not contrived any new
sins. Our heads have gathered more facts, but our hearts are beset
by the same worries and selfish concerns.

The other day I came across my copy of that wonderful story
by the Reverend Charles Dodgson, alias Lewis Carroll, called
Through the Looking Glass. Do you remember this sequel to *Alice
in Wonderland?* In it, Alice is playing in the parlor one day and
climbs up on the mantle above the fireplace to look into the large
mirror above it. But instead of seeing what one might expect, she
saw through the looking glass into another and wonderful world. Eventually Alice goes through the looking glass into that new world.

Scholars tell us that Alice, being in reality Lewis Carroll, sees
herself and comes to grips with herself in the characters and
situations she meets in that strange world. What a wonderful tale it
is.

Have you ever thought that it is possible to do precisely that
with the Bible? That you can go into it and walk around in it, find
it alive with all sorts of lovely and lusty characters who meet all
sorts of situations? Let me take you through the looking glass with
me today and see if you can see yourself (perhaps as others see
you) in this marvelous Bible of ours.

The interesting thing about walking around inside the Bible is that you can find people there that have the same doubts and questions you have. All sorts of people in the Bible have asked some of the "ultimate questions" of life and have struggled with answers.

Suppose your question is the big, basic one, the question about God. You yourself know the experience of a longing and a seeking after what is final and sure, and the haunting sense, which may never take a clear form with you but it's still there, that something is beyond you. Take that experience of longing, that leaning forward to look through the mists that cover the earth, to see if there is any real life beyond it. That is everyone's experience sometime.

Look over there. There is Abraham and Sarah, talk to them. Abraham is the one who had the impulse to leave his homeland which was safe and secure and where he was a reasonably wealthy person and go to a place that he didn't know anything about. Talk to him.

He tells you that something was driving him out. You have felt like that at some time in your life; you felt an urge to go out on some mission, undertake some task, or attack some great need, perhaps as aa compulsion so strong that it seemed to come from outside yourself. Was it God calling? Was Yahweh pushing you? Talk to Abraham.

With Abraham it becomes clear eventually. Abraham says that after a lot of frustration, doubt, and despair, he finally come to know "beyond the shadow of a doubt." Is there something in that account that rings true to you? Isn't there something here that you have half felt, half wanted to feel? It's tantalizing.

Or go over there and talk to Job. Job fought that battle in a different way. There seemed to be no misfortune or affliction that didn't overtake poor Job. Look at him sitting there: his fortune gone; his real estate wiped out; his children killed; stricken with a painful infection; and then he was given the ultimate curse, a nagging wife. We seem to forget that. After all is said and done, there is Mrs. Job standing beside him saying, "Curse God and die Job, curse God and die." What a comfort she was!

Yet, through it all, Job insisted on a troubled but repeated gamble of faith that God was somehow going to bring it out well. Doubts came up in his own mind, so that in the midst of clinging to his faith he would cry out, "Oh, that I knew where I might find Yahweh!"

Well, that's the kind of struggle of which life is made. You've probably known some of it. You want to believe, but these things you cannot understand. So you send up trembling questions again and again. And then, in the end, you hear Job saying: "I have heard of you by the hearing of the ear, but now my eyes have seen you." And somehow you know his experience is real, because you, too, have had that experience.

Or maybe you understand old Hanna standing over there, unable to have a child and wanting one so much, praying for one so hard that the priest thought that there was something wrong with her.

Or maybe you see yourself in Athens and you hear all the philosophical questions being asked of your beliefs. Look at that man coming up to those sophisticated teachers, his head balding, his eyes bright. Paul is his name, and he speaks with an authority about truth that comes not from books but from life experience. Some believe him and others laugh, and you know this is real for this has been your experience too.

You run into King David and you remember the story of David, Bathsheba, and Uriah, her husband. You remember what Nathan the prophet did after David's sin, how he pointed to David and said bluntly, "You are the one," and you know you can't get away from that kind of prophetic judgment; it's been meant for you.

Look at that crew standing over there, Giddeon, Isaiah, Moses, Jeremiah. Every single one of them was called to do a specific task by Yahweh, each said he was unfit to do the job, pleaded that he was not qualified, but in the end went and did. And the life of the human race has not been the same. Its been richer for their service.

As you move around in this wonderland of the Bible, you run into Thomas, the reluctant friend of Jesus. Talk to him for a while, and you will identify with him. "There I am. I just can't feel the rushing, unquestioning enthusiasm of the other Christians. Frankly, I'm skeptical, I've got to be shown, I'm like you, Thomas." But stand there another minute and you will see Thomas looking squarely at Jesus and, in a surge of faith, giving himself wholly to Jesus. And the transparent honesty of his former doubt turns the light on you to ask if you really are like that or not.

Ah, there is Peter. Follow him in your mind with his impulsive loyalty and impetuous acts of faithfulness. Then through his complete misunderstanding of Jesus to his weakness and his denial. And you say, "There I am, I'm like you, Peter. I mean well, but I make mistakes. I love Peter, he's so much like me." But then, all of a sudden, Peter stands there publicly calling upon men and women to repent and follow Jesus. Is that you? Daring to cross over racial lines at the risk of all his friendships, is that you? Finally giving up his life for the Christ, is that you?

If you wander around a little further in this book, a ragged face may come up to you with a pained expression of compassion. It is James, the brother of Jesus. He looks you right in the face and says:

> Suppose a brother or a sister is in rags with not enough food for the day, and one of you says, "Good luck to you, keep yourself warm, and have plenty to eat," but does nothing to supply their bodily needs. What is the good of that? So with faith, if it does not lead to action, is in itself a lifeless thing. [1]

Do you dare to talk to Pilate over there? Watch him try to rid himself of responsibility. Is that you?

Walk around in this book. Walk around in this wonderland and you will find little persons counting for much. Perhaps you see yourself in the fisherman, or the tax collector, or the educated defender of the old traditions, or the woman of all work in the house, or the woman who was the seller of purple. We are all there. Dreams are born in these pages. The people in darkness see a great light. The day-star begins to rise. There are voices calling, "Come over and help us." And you cannot help but feel the hope and the thrust of something big.

Here is a teacher, confidently sending a ragged group of friends out to establish a worldwide kingdom.

Here is a single missionary, claiming the whole Mediterranean world as his parish.

Here is an old man with a vision of youth looking on the triumphant achievement of the Kingdom of God and singing:

---

[1] James 2:15-17.

I saw a new heaven and a new earth . . . I saw the
holy city, new Jerusalem, coming down out of heaven from
God, made ready like a bride adorned for her husband . . .
I heard a loud voice proclaiming from the throne: "Now at
last God has his dwelling among men!" He will dwell
among them and they shall be his people, and God himself
will be with them. He will wipe every tear from their
eyes; there shall be an end to death, and to mourning and
crying and pain; for the old order has passed away! [2]

You see, I do find myself in this Bible! I can read this book
not simply as the story of many persons, but as my story. These
sins are my sins, these follies are my follies, these joys and sorrows
are my joys and sorrows. The warnings uttered are uttered to me.
The rebukes given are given to me. What is there here that I
cannot make my own?

What did Adam do that I have not done? I too have hidden in
the garden from the presence of my creator. I too like Esau have
sold my birthright for a mess of pottage. I too have reported that
the land of promise is too difficult to be possessed. I too have
clamored for the golden calf, and I too have disclaimed responsibility for having made it. I too have fled in fear from Jezebel and
have hidden in the cave at Horeb, only to be haunted there by a
sound of gentle stillness.

I too have demanded that the prophet be driven from the altar,
it was so much more comfortable to be soothed by the droning
priest. Many a time I have tempted the Nazarite to evil, lest by his
austere living he disturb me. Many a time like Jonah I have turned
my back on a Nineveh I hated and have taken a ship from Joppa to
Tarshish to escape, albeit in vain, the voice of conscience.

I am the priest and the levite who pass by the stricken
traveler. I hear the shocked exclamation, "This man receives sinners
and eats with them," and I recognize my own voice. I am the
prodigal son and the older brother as well. I protest the waste of
the gift of love offered by the woman at the feet of Jesus, because
I covet the gift for myself. I hide my talent in the ground. I tell
my soul to take its ease, to drink and be merry. I covet the best
place in what I take to be the Kingdom, one more of the sons of

---

2 Revelation 21:1-4.

Zebudee. As I listen to the prayer of the Pharisee, I know I am listening to myself.

I am in the crowd that shouts, "Hosanna," and as willingly I am in the crowd that shouts, "Crucify him, we have no king but Caesar." I am one of the solders who cast lots for the seamless robe that was patiently woven by the fingers of Mary. And when the Lord is laid in the tomb I help roll the stone to keep him there to trouble me no more. If I do not stone Stephen, I at least hold the garments of those who do.

Where in this book do I not find myself? Someone who knows me with an intimacy that is sheerly incredible has here written my autobiography. Each of these men and women is other than I, yet in each of them I see something of myself reflected. A voice thunders at me, "Thou art the man." And I know that the voice speaks truly and I respond, "It is I indeed."

But I look again and I am Abraham with the courage to be a pioneer. I am Miriam vowing to lead the people with Moses out of bondage across the sea and desert to a new land. I am Calib claiming Hebron for an inheritance, fortifications and giants not withstanding. I am Elijah standing up to a thousand false prophets. I am David celebrating and dancing before the Ark of the Lord. I am Esther setting the people of Israel free to return to their homeland.

I am one of the simple folk, who knew instinctively something magnificent was happening in a stable on a star filled night. I am the Samaritan stooping over the ragged wounded man.

Some people gather in an upstairs room off a narrow street, and into my hands are placed bread and a cup, and a voice speaks to me, "This is my body . . . this is my blood given for you."

I am racing from the garden tomb shouting, "He lives." I am on a ship taking the message to the world. I am saying:

> Victory is ours through him who loved us. For I am convinced that there is nothing in death or life, in the realm of spirits or superhuman powers, in the world as it is or the world as it shall be, in the forces of the universe, in heights or depths--nothing in all creation

that can separate us from the love of God in Christ Jesus
our Lord. [3]

Ah, but now I step back out through the looking glass and
once more I am in a hard, realistic, work-a-day world. Is it all a
wild and foolish dream? No! If any word of truth has ever been
spoken surely it does sound in this book.

> For the word of God is alive and active. It cuts more
> keenly than any two-edged sword, piercing as far as the
> place where life and spirit, joints and marrow, divide. It
> sifts the purposes and thoughts of the heart. [4]

Something does happen. Yahweh does move in that wonderland
of the Bible. But Yahweh also moves in this wonderland, in my
wonderland, in your wonderland of this present good earth, in this
present time when you live. That is the good news you find as you
walk about there and also in this place. Believe it.

"Repent" comes the cry from so many. Change your mind your
attitude. Throw away your old stethoscope and find a new way of
hearing the heartbeat of the future already pulsating in the community of the faithful and join it.

You who have ears, hear it. You who have eyes, see it. And
believe! Come alive and live as part of this faith community!

---

[3] Romans 8:37-39.

[4] Hebrews 4:12-13.